Garland English Texts

Stephen Orgel
Editor

Jerome McGann
Associate Editor

ENGLANDS ELIZABETH
by Thomas Heywood

edited by
Philip R. Rider

Garland English Texts
Number 8

GARLAND PUBLISHING, INC.
NEW YORK & LONDON
1982

Library of Congress Cataloging in Publication Data

Heywood, Thomas, d. 1641.
  Englands Elizabeth.

  (Garland English texts ; no. 8)
  Includes bibliographical references.
    1. Elizabeth I, Queen of England, 1533–1603.
  2. Great Britain—History—Elizabeth, 1558–1603.
  3. Great Britain—Kings and rulers—Biography.
  I. Rider, Philip R., 1941–   II. Title.
  III. Series.
  DA356.H62   1982   942.05′5′0924 [B]   80-9004
  ISBN 0-8240-9402-6   AACR2

Printed on acid-free, 250-year-life paper
Manufactured in the United States of America

CONTENTS

For
my parents

ACKNOWLEDGMENTS

It is with more pleasure than obligation that I acknowledge here the help afforded me by Professor William P. Williams. In addition to his careful reading of and thoughtful comments about the present work, Professor Williams has, through active encouragement and through the example of sound scholarship, been more responsible for whatever is of value in this work than he is aware.

Three other faculty members of Northern Illinois University deserve special thanks. Professors Craig Abbott and Edward Herbert devoted much time to a careful reading of my work at various stages, and their questions and suggestions helped me to avoid any number of pitfalls, large and small. Professor Philip Dust graciously checked (and almost invariably had to correct) my Latin translations.

A number of persons at other institutions also gave generously of their time. Miss Katharine Pantzer of the Houghton Library, Harvard University, provided me with information about several items in the revised *STC*. The following persons checked variant readings in copies of the 1631 edition of *Englands Elizabeth* for me; many of them sent detailed notes on the readings, a few sent photocopies, and all of them devoted no little effort to answering a stranger's questions: Dr. Margaret M. Wright (John Rylands Library, University of Manchester); Mr. Thomas V. Lange (Pierpont Morgan Library); Miss Christina M. Hanson (Beinecke Rare Book and Manuscript Library, Yale University); Mr. Wayne G. Hammond (Chapin Library, Williams College); L. W. Riley (Van Pelt Library, University of Pennsylvania); Dr. Nati H. Krivatsy (Folger Shakespeare Library); Mr. William Matheson (Rare Book and Special Collections Divison, Library of Congress); Oswalda Deva (Department of Special Collections, Stanford University Libraries); and Ms. Diane

Haack (who checked the Huntington Library copy). A few other librarians also deserve mention, specifically the staff of the Rare Book Room of the Newberry Library, and the Inter-Library Loan departments of Northern Illinois University and the University of Illinois at Chicago Circle.

Finally, a special word of gratitude goes to Professor Stephen Orgel of Johns Hopkins University who first suggested this work for publication.

INTRODUCTION

By the time Englands Elizabeth was published in 1631,
Thomas Heywood had already been a professional writer for
approximately thirty-seven years.[1] The first work which can
definitely be ascribed to him is The First and Second partes
of King Edward the Fourth, published in 1599. He was certainly writing before this date, however, because in 1598 Francis
Meres included him in a list of writers described as "the best
for Comedy,"[2] and on 14 October 1596 Henslowe recorded a loan
to four actors for the purchase of "hawodes bocke."[3] His earliest work may be the poem Oenone and Paris (1594), ascribed
on the title-page to "T. H." and unknown until it was sold at
Sotheby's in 1925, which has been accepted as Heywood's by
most modern scholars.[4] By 1631 he had published several
poems, including the enormous Troia Brittanica (1609), and
had either written or collaborated upon a number of plays--in
1633 he would claim to have "had either an entire hand, or at
the least a maine finger" in two hundred and twenty plays.[5]
He also had published translations of Ovid's de Arte Amandi
and of Sallust. His only prose work before Englands Elizabeth
was An Apology for Actors (1612).

Except for A Woman Killed With Kindness, a small handful
of other plays, and An Apology for Actors, Heywood is no
longer read. Most of the prose, the non-dramatic poetry,
and the translations have not been edited, and some of the
pieces have not even been reprinted since their first appearance in the seventeenth century. Chang and Hammersmith, com-
menting on the general state of Heywood criticism, say that
"his acknowledged high-quality works are frequently stressed
at the expense of a large body of lesser material which re-
ceives mention only in biographical or historical treatments.
Such unbalanced critical attention often results in a dis-
torted picture of Heywood's literary accomplishments."[6]
Englands Elizabeth has not received, so far as I know, the
attention of a single critical article devoted exclusively to
it. When the work is mentioned at all it usually appears
only as a title in a list of "Other Works," or it is noted as
a prose rendering of the play If You Know Not Me, You Know No
Bodie, part I (1605). Clark's standard critical book on Hey-

wood devotes one long paragraph (pp. 107-10) to Englands
Elizabeth, but except for a one-sentence statement on sources,
it confines itself wholly to identifying a few of the persons
named in the preliminary matter. The only genuinely positive
comments I have seen are such overstatements that they verge
on parody, referring to Englands Elizabeth as "that piece of
exquisite prose" and "[Heywood's] little masterpiece."[7] It
is unquestionably just that the bulk of critical attention be
directed to the plays--they are generally of a higher literary quality than are the prose and poetry. But Heywood obviously felt that these other works were important too, and
probably for more than just the income they might bring him.
Englands Elizabeth deserves more notice than it has received,
in part because it constitutes one small portion of the canon
of a writer of some importance, but also because it has some
merit of its own.

Heywood makes no claim to being a historian, despite the
number of historical plays and popular histories he wrote.
He seems instead to have viewed himself as a "popularizer,"
though without the pejorative connotations which the modern
reader associates with that term. In his address to the
reader in The Life of Merlin (Wing H1786; 1641)--a "popular"
history of Britain--Heywood explains exactly what he is trying to do. He is going to provide the reader with

> a true catalogue of all the Kings of this Island,
> with a summary of all passages of State Ecclesias-
> ticall or Temporall, of any remarke or moment,
> during their Principalities and Dominions, in so
> much that scarce anything shall be here wanting to
> thy best wishes, if thou beest desirous to be in-
> structed, and faithfully informed in the knowledge
> of our English Annalls.
>
> [sigs.¶ 4r-v]

This is perfectly straightforward and commonplace; it could
have come from the pen of any seventeenth-century writer of
popular history. It explains that the book will combine the
ideals of completeness and selectivity by offering "all the
Kings" and "all passages of State," but in "summary" fashion,
thus fulfilling the "best wishes" of its readers. Heywood
goes on to explain, however, that his book will differ from
other histories because he has tried to be considerate of his
audience:

> For in the steed of a large study book, and huge
> voluminous Tractate, able to take up a whole yeare
> in reading, and to load and tyre a Porter in carry-

ing, thou hast here a small Manuell, containing all
the pith and marrow of the greater, made portable
for thee (if thou so please) to beare in thy pocket,
so that thou mayst say, that in this small compen-
dium or abstract, thou hast Hollinshed, Polychroni-
con, Fabian, Speed, or any of the rest, of more
Giantlike bulke or binding. . . .

[sig.¶ 4v]

Another and perhaps more telling indication of Heywood's
awareness of his audience is found in his address to the
reader of Gunaikeion; or, Nine Bookes of Various History.
Concerninge Women (STC 13326; 1624). After explaining that
he has chosen the women in his book either for their virtues
which the seventeenth-century woman should emulate or for
their vices which his audience should avoid, he adds that he
has included some humorous stories to balance the serious
ones, because "they that write to all, must strive to please
all" (sig. A4v). To the modern reader, this statement suggests that such blatant crowd-pleasing efforts can produce
only a slipshod and superficial book. To Heywood's credit,
however, his ready admission that he is a popularizer trying
"to please all" makes his intentions seem, if not altruistic,
at least somewhat less pecuniary and shallow.

Heywood's motive for writing popular history seems to
have been that "he was cognizant of the value of history for
its patriotic teaching and wished to present it in a brief
and accurate form for the benefit of the general public."8
In Englands Elizabeth he alludes to the purpose of his work
when he scolds those "Criticks" who "will not or dare not
. . . adventure the expence of one serious hower in any
laborious worke intended for the benefit of either Church or
Common-weale" (ll. 62-65). Specifically, Heywood was interested in two audiences which had been largely ignored before
the mid-seventeenth century. The educated reader of the
seventeenth century could turn to a number of sources for
historical fact, but these were generally large, expensive
books often written in Latin and often weighted down with
scholarly apparatus. For his moral instruction, this same
educated reader could turn to the rich and varied allegorical
literature or to any number of theological treatises. But
Heywood was looking to the audience that wanted to know something of history, that wanted the "lesson" history could
teach, but that could not acquire these in very many other
books. He was also concerned with women readers. Few
writers before Heywood considered that the middle-class woman
might want something more edifying and enlightening than
practical books of cookery or plague remedies, sermons and

religious pamphlets, or sensational broadsides. Some of his remarks about women (see _Englands Elizabeth_, 11. 655-63) are typical of their time, and I am not here trying to make a case for Heywood as an early "liberator" of women or a zealot for women's rights, but Louis B. Wright is no doubt correct when he states that Heywood was "perhaps woman's staunchest literary advocate in the first half of the seventeenth century, [and he] was convinced of her capacity to read and appreciate."[9]

F. Smith Fussner characterizes Heywood as perhaps "the most interesting and successful of all the popularizers of history writing in the early seventeenth century," but Fussner misjudges both the author and his audience when he adds that "Heywood was simply a more able and amusing writer than most who catered to the popular taste for gossip in the plain wrapper of history."[10] Heywood was, to all appearances, trying to write history; if what he presented occasionally included "gossip" it was gossip that had been accepted as historical fact not only by Heywood but by more distinguished historians such as Holinshed. _Englands Elizabeth_ could certainly have been made much more sensational or much more didactic, but Heywood generally resisted both impulses. It would be inaccurate to term Heywood a "historian," but there is little doubt that he took his history writing seriously and that he was more than a mere exploiter of the ever-present market for sensationalism. Wright's assessment of him is clear and accurate:

> Among the Elizabethans, Thomas Heywood stands out in his effort to make literature easily understood by the commonality of readers. In him there is no despising of the intelligence of the bourgeoisie. In his serious productions he seeks to provide such explanatory equipment as will make clear all obscurities or difficult allusions. All of this he does without condescension, in a frank attempt to make enlightenment easy. Nowhere is Heywood's endeavor to popularize knowledge more apparent than in his historical and historical-biographical works.[11]

Judged as popular history, with all the necessary limitations of that genre, _Englands Elizabeth_ is, I think, successful. According to Herschel Baker, there were two widely-held Renaissance notions about the writing of history: the historian "has a special obligation to ascertain and state the truth of things," and "such truths are exemplary."[12] How far did Heywood go in trying to "ascertain . . . the truth of things"?

He did what is required of the good writer of popular his-
tory--he went not to any "primary" research materials, but to
the recognized secondary authorities, in this case Foxe and
Holinshed. Many renaissance historians who thought of themselves as historians did no more. And Heywood obviously attempted to represent his authorities accurately. This in
itself demonstrates a good deal of resistance to temptation
when one considers the story Heywood was working with: a
princess, born of a mother unjustly executed for treason,
grows into an intelligent, sensitive young girl; she is persecuted and attempts are made on her life by an evil sister
and the sister's allies; the princess survives by her determination and her devotion to God, until one day the sister
dies and the princess becomes queen. And, as every reader
knew, the queen became England's greatest monarch. Had Heywood been merely a sensationalizer, he could have altered the
story in many ways (as other writers, through the present day,
have done) to depict a more pathetic Elizabeth, a more sinister and conniving Mary, and a crueller Bedingfield--in short,
to exploit the obvious dramatic elements in the story. He
chose not to do this, however, but instead to stick to the
facts as he knew them. As I will try to show later, Heywood
made somewhat selective use of his sources but he seldom de-
viated from or contradicted them.

Worship of Elizabeth was fairly commonplace during the
sixteenth and seventeenth centuries,[13] and Heywood seems
to have been one of those most seriously stricken by the
idolatry. In an age when the work of most historians was,
despite their obligation to the truth, colored by political,
religious, and/or personal convictions,[14] Heywood has not
allowed his bias seriously to intrude into Englands
Elizabeth. Elizabeth, Edward, and their friends and allies
are, of course, the sympathetic figures, while Henry VIII,
Mary, Stephen Gardiner, and Henry Bedingfield are the vil-
lains. But unlike Foxe, for example, he has not shown the
opposing camps of Catholic and Protestant in stark black and
white; instead he has attempted to maintain a certain balance,
to present a favorable picture of Elizabeth without a fervid
denunciation of the Catholics.[15] His description of Mary's
death, for example, is almost touching in its recounting of
her final lonely hours, with her husband gone and the responsibility for Calais heavy on her mind. He makes a point
of saying that the troubles and oppression during her reign
were not entirely her fault but were caused by "the blind
zeale of her Religion, and authority of the clergy" (11. 2523-
24). He also displays his equitability when he quashes the
"gossip" that Jane Grey was pregnant at the time of her execution by declaring that "her Romish opposites . . . would not

use such inhumanity against so great a person" (11. 1046-49).
Heywood also allows us to see, but only for a moment, a not-
so-pleasant side of Elizabeth when, upon her being taken to
the Tower, she addresses her sympathetic gentleman usher in
peevish, selfish anger (11. 1471-76).

Heywood's prose style is well suited to the writing of
history: it is an undistinguished style, lacking "the collo-
quial vigor, the color, the gusto, that we think of as typical
of the best [Elizabethan] prose."[16] Renaissance historians
"were, if not afraid of style, at any rate suspicious of its
charms as hostile to instruction,"[17] and thus they "resisted
elegance, and most of them remained committed to what Ascham
called a 'playne and open' style."[18] Holinshed, for example,
states that his "speech is plaine, without any rhetoricall
shew of eloquence, having rather a regard to simple truth,
than to decking words."[19] Although it contains a few of the
archaic or peculiar words of which Heywood was fond, the vo-
cabulary of Englands Elizabeth generally avoids the Latinate
terms with which he sometimes sprinkles his plays. His sentences have a tendency to ramble,[20] but except for an occasional short flight into euphuistic alliteration and balance
(see 11. 1915-16, 2422-30, 2553-54),[21] the prose is clear and
readily understandable; there are no allegorical passages or
extended metaphors to obscure the sense and confuse the
reader. When the language becomes figurative, the images are
commonplace and easily understood, most of them deriving from
nature: "Her life was a continuall warfare, like a ship in the
middst of an Irish sea" (11. 2413-14); "The Cloud thus set,
that wished Sunne appeared in our horizon like a fresh spring
after a stormy winter" (2534-36); "Shee swamme to the Crowne
through a Sea of Sorrow" (1135). Other images are drawn from
a variety of ordinary sources including the Bible and sport
(11. 1119-21).

Perhaps the most vivid language in Englands Elizabeth is
that used in describing the fire at Woodstock (11. 1930-35).
The movement of the image from a relatively small house fire
to the execution fires of the Protestant martyrs (with a bit
of word play on "bonfires"), and then to the nation and the
world in flame, and ultimately to God "whose breath is as a
flaming fire" (1946), is powerful and effective. The repetition of the word Fire and the series of short balanced
phrases provide a sense of relentless movement and eventual
engulfment. And "in the midst of that fiery tryall" stands
Elizabeth, simultaneously the focal point and the victim,
whose rescue (and, symbolically, that of the hope of England)
is effected only by divine providence. The fire with which
"fiery Adversaries" are "blasted" reappears at line 2350 in
the "inflammation" of Gardiner's final illness, and the jus-

tice of his death is pointed out in the sidenote: "Gardiner had enflamed many Martyrs, and hath now his body enflamed." For Heywood, the fire at Woodstock obviously had great symbolic value; his description provides it with a climactic intensity which its context in the narrative does not support. Frederick S. Boas's description of Heywood's prose style in Gunaikeion is also appropriate to Englands Elizabeth:

> There are, no doubt, long jejune stretches where he was hurriedly dishing up traditional material. But . . . I would make the claim that Heywood showed remarkable skill in one of the most difficult of literary genres, the short story. And in his occasional reflective passages his style attains dignity and an impressively sombre rhythm. If after the fashion of his day, he was too fond of coining ponderous neologisms, he knew both in his poetry and his prose the value of the effect gained by mingling long, resonant and pithy monosyllabic words.[22]

Waith says of the prose of Exemplary Lives that it "is workmanlike, readable, and well-suited to narrative—far removed from the grandeur of epic but a natural development of the style of exemplary biography and popular history."[23] These comments suggest that a careful study of Heywood's prose style (a major desideratum in Heywood studies) would likely repay the time it would require.

There remains to be said something about the sources of Englands Elizabeth. Heywood is a rich mine for source studies because he borrowed freely and extensively from a wide range of authors; Robert Grant Martin found no less than fifty-seven ancient and modern writers which Heywood used, either directly or through an intermediary source, in Gunaikeion,[24] and there has been a rather large amount of scholarship devoted to discovering the sources of the plays. In addition, Heywood quite often re-used his own material, or material he had borrowed, in later works. Much of Englands Elizabeth appeared first as If You Know Not Me, part I; the play was very popular, going through eight editions between 1605 and 1639,[25] and is nearly identical in narrative and occasionally in language to Englands Elizabeth. The following comparison is typical:[26]

> Winch: It is the pleasure of her maiestie,
>   That you be straight committed to the Tower.
> Eliz: The Tower, for what?
> Winch: Moreouer all your howshold seruants we haue
>   (discharged,

> Except this gentleman your vsher & this gentlewoman
> Thus did the Queene commaund,
> And for your guard, a hundred Northern whitecotes,
> Are appoynted to conduct you thither,
> To night vnto your chamber, to morrow early prepare
> You for the Tower. . . .
> [If You Know Not Me, 11. 440-49] [27]

> Gardiner and the rest entred the Chamber and told her
> that it was her Majesties pleasure shee must instantly
> bee conveyed to the Tower, that her houshold was
> dissolved, and all her servants discharged, except her
> Gentleman Usher, three Gentle-women, and two Groomes,
> and that for her guard two hundred Northern white Coates
> were appointed that night to watch about her lodging,
> and early in the morning to see her safely delivered
> into the custody of the Lieftenant of the Tower.
> [Englands Elizabeth, 11. 1335-45]

Heywood then used much of the biographical information and
much of the language of Englands Elizabeth for the sections
about Elizabeth in The Exemplary Lives and memorable Acts of
nine the most worthy Women of the World (1640) and, the following year, in The Life of Merlin.[28]

Most of If You Know Not Me is drawn from Foxe's Acts and
Monuments with some minor matters taken from Holinshed.[29]
For Englands Elizabeth, Heywood went back to these sources,
drawing most of the biographical information about Elizabeth
from Foxe and most of the other material from Holinshed (some
of which no doubt reached him via Henry Holland; see 11. 94-
102). In many places, Heywood "borrowed" verbatim:

> It would make a pitiful and a strange story, here by the
> way to touch and recite what examination and rackings of
> poor men there were, to find out that knife that should
> cut her throat.
>
> [Foxe] [30]

> It would make a pittiful and strange Story, to relate
> what examinations and rackings of poore men there was to
> finde but out that knife which might cut her throat.
> [Englands Elizabeth, 11. 1645-48]

There are many such passages. Heywood seems to have followed
his sources most closely when he was reproducing speeches,
perhaps feeling that Foxe (or someone before him) had recorded the words accurately and that they were not to be tampered
with; compare the following versions of one of the encounters

between Elizabeth and Henry Bedingfield:

> "None of them durst be so bold," he trowed, "to carry
> her letters, being in that case." "Yes," quoth she, "I
> am assured I have none so dishonest that would deny my
> request in that behalf, but will be as willing to serve
> me now as before." "Well," said he, "my commission is
> to the contrary, and I may not so suffer it." Her
> grace, replying again, said, "You charge me very often
> with your commission; I pray God, you may justly answer
> the cruel dealing you use towards me."
>
> [Foxe, VIII, 617]

> I hope there is none of your Servants dares be so bold
> as to deliver any Letters of yours to her Majestie, you
> being in that case. Yes (quoth shee) I have none that
> are so dishonest, but will be as willing to doe for me
> in that behalfe, as ever they were. That's true (said
> he) but my Commission is to the contrary; I can by no
> means suffer it. Her Grace replying againe, said, You
> charge mee very often with your Commission, I pray God
> you may hereafter answer the cruell dealing used towards
> mee.   [Englands Elizabeth, ll. 2016-26]

It is important to note that Heywood's borrowing is selective.
He does not follow Holinshed's account of Henry beyond Anne
Boleyn, except to account for his death and his will. He
goes to Foxe for the story of Gardiner's death, but he does
not get sidetracked into the story of Latimer and Ridley.
Heywood is obviously making selective use of his sources and
is not simply copying passages at random.

Except for the statement about Henry Holland, only in one
other place does Heywood actually mention his authority--in
the sidenote "Fox. acts and Monuments" (opposite line 2320) at
the beginning of the paragraph describing Gardiner's final
hours. He alludes several times (ll. 297-98, 1390, 2324,
e.g.) to the fact that he is working from sources, however,
and makes one direct statement of the fact (ll. 648-49), so
there is no reason to suppose that he was trying to conceal
either his sources or the use he made of them. After all, by
seventeenth-century standards, he was not plagiarizing, but
was merely relying on reputable authority.[31] Foxe and Holinshed were not Heywood's only authorities (see the Explanatory
Note to ll. 644-70), but they were the primary ones, and I
have made no attempt to identify the source of every bit of
information in Englands Elizabeth; given the amount and nature
of the borrowing done by early historians, such a task would
be enormously complex.

It is fair to say, I think, that <u>Englands Elizabeth</u> filled a need. It seems to have been the first separate account in English of Elizabeth's early years.[32] It tells its story directly and clearly, without sermonizing, without long digressions, and without attempting to explore complex issues. And, perhaps most importantly, it appeared in a size and at a price that made it easily available to a rapidly-increasing reading public.

Notes

1. The standard biography and one of the best book-length critical studies of Heywood is Arthur Melville Clark's Thomas Heywood: Playwright and Miscellanist (1958; rpt New York: Russell, 1967).

2. Palladis Tamia, sig. Oo3v. Bentley undercuts Meres's praise by calling it "a suggestive example of Meres's lack of discrimination" (G. E. Bentley, The Jacobean and Caroline Stage, IV [Oxford: Clarendon Press, 1956], 554).

3. Although it occasionally needs correcting and augmenting, Clark's "A Bibliography of Thomas Heywood," Oxford Bibliographical Society Proceedings & Papers, 1 (1922-26), 97-153, conveniently collects the entries for Heywood in Henslowe's Diary, the Revels' Accounts, Sir Henry Herbert's Office-Book, and the Stationers' Register.

4. See Joseph Quincy Adams, ed., Oenone and Paris (Washington: Folger, 1943). Adams's attribution of the work to Heywood has not been questioned; nevertheless, Miss Katharine Pantzer has informed me that it will be listed in the revised STC under the heading "T. H." (STC 12578.5).

5. "To the Reader," The English Traveller, in The Dramatic Works of Thomas Heywood, ed. R. H. Shepherd (1874; rpt. New York: Russell, 1964), IV, 5.

6. Joseph S. M. J. Chang and James P. Hammersmith, "Thomas Heywood," in The Popular School: A Survey and Bibliography of Recent Studies in English Renaissance Drama, ed. Terence P. Logan and Denzell S. Smith (Lincoln: Univ. of Nebraska Press, 1975), p. 110. This is the best secondary bibliography of Heywood; it is supplemented by Otto Rauchbauer, "Thomas Heywood: An Annotated Bibliography, 1967--," Research Opportunities in Renaissance Drama, 18 (1975), 45-50, and by Philip R. Rider, "Thomas Heywood: A Supplementary, Annotated Bibliography, 1966-1975," RORD, 19 (1976), 33-36.

7. Charles Whibley, "Introduction," The Conspiracy of Catiline and the War of Jugurtha, by Sallust, trans. Thomas Heywood (London: Constable, 1924), pp. xvii, xix.

8. Louis B. Wright, "Heywood and the Popularizing of History," Modern Language Notes, 43 (1928), 288.

9. _Middle-Class Culture in Elizabethan England_ (1935; rpt. Ithaca, N. Y.: Cornell Univ. Press, 1958), p. 117.

10. _The Historical Revolution: English Historical Writing and Thought 1580-1640_ (London: Routledge and Kegan Paul, 1962), p. 184. Robert Grant Martin, in "A Critical Study of _Gunaikeion_," _Studies in Philology_, 20 (1923), 163, reaches the opposite conclusion: he finds that Heywood has tried to present honest, factual information and has not merely repeated lurid stories.

11. "Heywood and the Popularizing of History," 287. Lest Wright be thought merely an apologist for Heywood, it should be noted that in another place he includes him with Greene, Deloney, Dekker, and Samuel Rowlands as one of those who "turned their hands to anything that would bring in a penny" (_Middle-Class Culture_, pp. 436-37).

12. _The Race of Time: Three Lectures on Renaissance Historiography_ (Toronto: Univ. of Toronto Press, 1967), p. 16.

13. For a full discussion of the dedication to and virtual deification of Elizabeth, see Elkin Calhoun Wilson, _England's Eliza_ (1939; rpt. New York: Octagon, 1966), and Frances A. Yates, "Queen Elizabeth as Astraea," _Journal of the Warburg and Courtauld Institutes_, 10 (1947), 27-82 (rpt. in _Astrea: The Imperial Theme in the Sixteenth Century_ [London: Routledge & Kegan Paul, 1975], pp. 29-87).

14. Baker, p. 24.

15. Of _1 If You Know Not Me_ Frederick S. Boas writes: "The favourable light in which the foreign and Roman Catholic king [Philip] is shown is one of the most striking features of the play. This is all the more remarkable because it closes with a ringing Protestant panegyric on the open Bible from the lips of Elizabeth. . . ." See _An Introduction to Stuart Drama_ (Oxford: Oxford Univ. Press, 1946), p. 175.

16. Martin, "A Critical Study of _Gunaikeion_," 183. Writing about Heywood's _Exemplary Lives and memorable Acts of nine the most worthy Women_ (1640), Eugene M. Waith says: "Heywood was enough of a scholar to know that traditional rhetorical decorum prescribed a low style for such an enterprise" ("Heywood's Women Worthies," in _Concepts of the Hero in the Middle Ages and the Renaissance_, ed. Norman T. Burns and Christopher J. Reagan [Albany: State Univ. of New

York Press, 1975], p. 230). Similarly, Madeleine Doran says, of Heywood's domestic tragedies: "It was evidently felt . . . that decorum demanded a plain style . . ." (Endeavors of Art: A Study of Form in Elizabethan Drama [Madison: Univ. of Wisconsin Press, 1954], p. 145).

17. Baker, p. 88.

18. Ibid., p. 86.

19. Raphael Holinshed, Holinshed's Chronicles of England, Scotland, and Ireland, ed. Henry Ellis (1808; rpt. New York: AMS, 1965), II, [ix].

20. How much of this is what Heywood intended and how much is due to the printer's treatment of his copy is impossible to determine. See the Textual Introduction.

21. Heywood has been described as being "childishly fond of . . . balancing with aliteration," by Joseph Quincy Adams, Jr., "The Authorship of A Warning for Fair Women," PMLA, 28 (1913), 598; cf., e.g., "Esay, but a saw" (1. 1979), and "wage no warre, nor giue no warriours wages" (Oenone and Paris, 1. 421).

22. Thomas Heywood (1950; rpt. New York: Phaeton Press, 1975), pp. 119-20.

23. Waith, p. 230.

24. "A Critical Study of Gunaikeion," 165-77.

25. See Clark, "A Bibliography of Thomas Heywood," 102-04.

26. Shepherd lists a number of other parallel passages in Dramatic Works, I, 361-77.

27. The Malone Society reprint, ed. Madeleine Doran (Oxford: Oxford Univ. Press, 1935).

28. In 1639 appeared a poem entitled "The life and death of Queene Elizabeth, From the wombe to the Tombe, from her Birth to her Buriall" (STC 7587), which Clark calls "a rude versifying of England's Elizabeth or a rhyming version of If You Know Not Me, part I" ("A Bibliography of Thomas Heywood," 133). Clark attributes the poem to Heywood, saying "such a plagiarizing of himself would be quite in

keeping with Heywood's practice." The attribution may be correct, but Heywood was capable of much better verse than this.

29. See Robert Grant Martin, "The Sources of Heywood's _If You Know Not Me, You Know Nobody_, Part I," _Modern Language Notes_, 39 (1924), 220-22.

30. John Foxe, _The Acts and Monuments of John Foxe_, ed. S. R. Cattley and George Townsend (1843-49; rpt. New York: AMS, 1965), VIII, 610. Parenthetical citations are to this edition.

31. Martin states that Heywood acknowledged his sources in _Gunaikeion_ as well as might be expected; see "A Critical Study of _Gunaikeion_," 177-78.

32. It may also have been the last until Alison Plowden's _The Young Elizabeth_ (Newton Abbot: Readers Union, 1972).

TEXTUAL INTRODUCTION

The printing history of Englands Elizabeth is not particularly complicated. Our first knowledge of the work is an entry for Philip Waterhouse in the Stationers' Register for 26 April 1631:

> Entred for his Copie vnder the handes of Master MARTIN and Master Kingston warden. a booke called Englandes ELIZABETH her Life and troubles dureinge her minoritye from the Cradle to the Crowne By T. H.[1]

The book first appeared sometime in 1631 as a twelvemo printed by John Beale for Waterhouse. A second edition, again a twelvemo and for Waterhouse but with no printer named, was called for in 1632. The last of the early editions, still in twelvemo, was printed in 1641 by Roger Daniel to be sold by John Sweeting. Not until 1813 did it appear again, rather heavily "modernized," this time in The Harleian Miscellany.[2] For more than another century and a half Englands Elizabeth remained out of print, until a photo-facsimile of the 1631 edition was issued in 1973.[3]

The title-page of the first edition is as follows:

> [within a frame of rectangular ornaments] ENGLANDS | ELIZABETH: | HER LIFE AND | TROVBLES, | During Her Minoritie, | from the Cradle to the | CROWNE. | Historically laid open and inter-| wouen with such eminent Passages | of STATE, as happened vnder the | Reigne of HENRY the Eight, EDVVARD | the Sixt, Q. MARY; all of them | aply introducing to the | present Relation. | [rule] | By THO: HEYWOOD. | [rule] | LONDON, | Printed by IOHN BEALE, for PHILIP | WATERHOVSE; and are to be sold at | his Shop at St. Pauls head, neere | London-stone. 1631. |

The first edition collates: A-L[12] [$5 (-A1-A4, B5, C5, E5) signed; I4 missigned A4]; 132 leaves, pp. [24] 1-230 213 232-234 [235-240] [=264]; 69 misnumbered 67 in uncorrected state. The contents are: A1r-A3r, blank; A3v, engraved

frontispiece; A4r, title-page; A4v, blank; A5r-A8v,
dedication; A9r-A12r, "TO THE | GENEROVS | READER."; A12v,
blank; B1r-L9v, text; L10r-L12v, blank. In the text the
running-head is in the formula: "[ruling monarch] Englands |
Elizabeth. An. [year]". The frontispiece is by Martin
Droeshout and is reproduced in Arthur M. Hind, Engraving in
England in the Sixteenth & Seventeenth Centuries, II
(Cambridge: Cambridge Univ. Press, 1955), plate 214(b). It
measures 121 x 67mm and depicts Elizabeth, with Woodstock in
the background, standing by a table upon which a Bible lies
open to Psalm 66:16--"O come hither & hearken all ye that
feare god & I will tell ye what he hath don for my soule."
From her mouth issues a banner with the words "If the Lord
had not bene on my side." Directly above Elizabeth's head
two cherubim bearing a crown descend; in the light of heaven
above them are the words "Many daughters have don well but
thou surpassest them all." Above the engraving is the motto
"Est mihi supplicij causa fuisse piam" and below the
engraving "I S. Invent."--presumably the engraver, but I
have been unable to identify him.

Each page, including those in the dedication and the
address "To the Reader," is outlined by a ruled box 123.5 x
66mm (sig. D2r), encompassing both the headline and the
direction line. There is another horizontal rule beneath
the headline and another vertical rule approximately one-
third of the way in from the outer edge of the frame, leaving a text "box" of 115 x 45mm and a space of 115 x 21mm for
the marginalia. On a typical page, twenty lines of type
fill 94 mm (D2r), while twenty lines in the marginal notes
occupy 68.5 mm (B8r).

The copy from which this edition was set was presumably
manuscript and may have been scribal rather than authorial.
Given the wretchedness of Heywood's hand and the incompetence
of Beale's compositors--I will be returning to these points
later--it is surprising not to find more evidence of compositorial misreading of the copy. Little is known about Heywood's preferences in such matters as punctuation, capitalization, and spelling;[4] in a somewhat cursory examination of the
only two manuscripts generally thought to be in Heywood's
hand (The Escapes of Jupiter and The Captives: Egerton MS
1994, fols. 52a-95), I have noticed only that there seems to
be a slight preference for "ee" in "he," "she," and "we," and
for the tilde to replace the nasals "n" and "m." Unfortunately, neither of these practices is rigidly adhered to in
the manuscripts nor can their presence in the printed work be
taken as firm evidence of the work having been set from Heywood's holograph copy. It was common practice in many
seventeenth-century printshops for the compositor to justify

his line by increasing or decreasing the number of terminal
es; the use of the tilde was less usual in 1631 than it had
been earlier, but we know that in Englands Elizabeth Beale
used it in this way when he stopped the press to try to correct "convenient" (see note to 1. 675 in the Textual Notes).

Two other factors also suggest the use of scribal copy.
Heywood knew that his handwriting was hard to read; at the
end of Exemplary Lives he asks the reader to excuse the errors because "the Compositor . . . received this Coppy in a
difficult and unacquainted hand" (sig. 2F4v).[5] This suggests that Heywood's printers usually received more legible
copy supplied either by Heywood making a careful copy of his
"foul papers" or by a professional copyist. It should, however, be remembered that 1631 was a busy year for Heywood
and that he may not have wished to devote part of his time
to transcribing a clean copy of his work. He had just been
appointed to write the Lord Mayor's pageant (Londons Ius
Honorarium), and he was preparing Sir Richard Barckley's
The Felicitie of Man (STC 1383; 1631) for the press.[6] It
is possible of course that Heywood prepared his own clean
copy for the printer; E. A. J. Honigmann has shown that
while The Captives is undoubtedly a holograph, the number
of typical copying errors indicate that Heywood was making
a fair copy of an earlier draft of the manuscript.[7]

John Beale seems to have been a generally careless work-
man, and the edition of 1631 is poorly printed.[8] Ben Jonson,
for whom Beale printed Bartholomew Fair, The Devil Is An
Asse, and The Staple of News, all in 1631, complained of him
in a letter to the Earl of Newcastle:

> It is the Lewd Printers fault, that I can send your
> Lordship, no more of my Booke [Staple of News] done.
> . . . Before he will perfect the rest, I feare, hee
> will come himselfe to be a part, under the title of the
> absolute knave, which he hath play'd with mee; My
> Printer, and I, shall afford subject enough for a
> Tragi-Comoedy. for with his delayes and vexation, I am
> almost become blind, and if Heaven be so just in the
> Metamorphosis, to turne him into that Creature hee most
> assimilates, a Dog with a Bell to lead mee betweene
> Whitehall and my lodging, I may bid the world good
> Night.[9]

The errors made in Beale's shop are numerous, and most of
them should have been readily noticeable to a proofreader:
added letters, dropped letters, duplicated words, omitted
words, confusing spacing, and gross misspellings (see the
emendation lists). There are also turned letters (a in

"tolerable," 1. 132; us in "Favourite," 1. 2106, and
"would," 1. 2290; n in "honourable," 1. 2195), letters in
wrong font ("Hen-|ry" at 1. 10), and pieces of type so badly
damaged as to be unreadable (in some copies "bewayling your"
at 1. 935 looks like "bewailing our"). Perhaps the most
characteristic error is the large number of repeated words,
usually arising from the compositor repeating at the beginning of a line the last word of the previous line (see, e.g.,
the textual notes to ll. 6 and 680, and the sidenote at 1.
174). In their examination of Beale's printing of the three
Jonson plays, Herford and Simpson found that "Beale made almost every mistake which a bad and careless printer was capable of making" (VI, 4) and characterized his work as "hasty
and slovenly" (VI, 149), with many "stupid and obvious
blunders" (VI, 274); the examples of errors they give show
them to be the same kind as one finds in Englands Elizabeth.
Herford and Simpson quote Beale's advice to the reader of
William Gouge's The Whole-Armour of God (1616) as illustrative
of his attitude toward his work and his customers: "If therefore thou meete with any slippe that may make the sence obscure, compare thy Booke with some others, and thou maiest
finde it amended" (VI, 8).

Beale seems to have had an adequate supply of type for
this relatively small book, but he ran short of a few special
characters. The very small area in which type is actually
set necessitated a great deal of hyphenation, and as a result,
one often finds the double hyphen, or "equals" sign, being
used, and in at least one case ("Child-bed" at 1. 505) a
period.

The sheets of Englands Elizabeth were imposed and folded
in the common way for a duodecimo; this is determined by the
horizontal chainlines and the appearance of the watermark at
the outer edge of leaves 11 and 12 of each sheet.[10] Beale
employed at least two and perhaps as many as five compositors
in 1631,[11] but an examination of nine pairs of words[12] for
spelling preferences yields no clear evidence that more than
one compositor set the book.

There is evidence, however, that two skeleton formes were
used in the setting of most of the book. The recto half of
each running-head reads "Elizabeth" with the appropriate date
following. On one page of each forme the reading is
"EliZabeth" with a swash capital "Z." In gatherings B and C
this distinctive running-head appears in the same relative
position in each forme--on 3r of the outers and 4r of the
inners. The use of this single skeleton (which I will desig-
nate "I") indicates that the work was going rather slowly in
these first gatherings; after the compositor locked up the
outer forme of B, for example, he had to wait for it to be

machined before he could set the inner forme. It is altogether likely that he was not really waiting but was instead
at work on another book, and the press, rather than standing
idle while another forme of Englands Elizabeth was being set,
was probably then running off the sheets of this other book.
When the outer forme of gathering D came to be set, a second
skeleton ("II") was made up: once again it had a swash "Z" in
one of the headlines, but it was a different and probably
newer piece of type with a much longer tail extending well
below the "a." This distinctive type also remains in the
same position in the forme, on 5r of the outers and 6r of the
inners. In gatherings D through L (the last) the two skeletons are used for each sheet; the formes seem to have been
printed in the following order:[13]

B(o)	B(i)	C(o)	C(i)	D(o)	D(i)	E(i)	E(o)	F(o)
I	I	I	I	II	I	II	I	I

F(i)	G(i)	G(o)	H(o)	H(i)	I(o)	I(i)	K(i)	K(o)
II	I	II	I	II	II	I	II	I

L(i)	L(o)
II	I

This order, alternating skeletons I and II, would seem to be
quite normal if one posits an interruption after E(o) and
another after H(i) to allow the same skeleton to be used for
two successive formes.

When the second edition of Englands Elizabeth appeared
in 1632 it was still owned by Philip Waterhouse but it was
printed, according to the title-page, in Cambridge. No
printer is named, but two of the three ornamental initials
(those at the beginning of the dedicatory epistle and of the
epistle to the reader) are identical with those used in the
1641 edition printed in Cambridge by Roger Daniel. Daniel
was appointed one of the printers to the University of
Cambridge on 24 July 1632, joining in partnership with
Thomas Buck.[14] The evidence of the initials suggests, but
certainly does not prove, that the 1632 edition was printed
by either Daniel or Buck.

The second edition is also a duodecimo, collating A-I[12].
The printing is clean and virtually error-free. A number of
changes, the more obvious of which can be attributed to the
printer, are introduced into this edition. It is not surprising, for example, to find that the old u/v and i/j usage
of 1631 has now been modernized; the 1630s were the time
during which this change was becoming widespread.[15] The
second edition puts into lower case the many capitalized

nouns of the first edition and makes somewhat more regular
use of italic. Spelling is also regularized to a considerable degree: words ending in "ee" usually have only a single
"e"; names such as "Westminster" and "Benningfield" are
spelled one way throughout; and "Elizabeth" is spelled every-
where, including the title-page, with an "s." Heywood's
spelling is so erratic and sometimes bizarre that it is difficult to imagine that he would have been concerned to carefully regularize it for the 1632 edition;16 the changes can,
with a high degree of certainty, be ascribed to the printer.

The source for another class of alterations in the
second edition is somewhat more doubtful. The change which
the modern reader first notices is the heavy and thorough
repunctuation. The new punctuation probably reflects the
imposition of a "house style" on the copy. Heywood himself
seems to have had little interest in such matters and no
doubt relied on the printer to take care of the pointing--a
common attitude in the sixteenth and seventeenth centuries.
Heywood's part in <u>Sir Thomas More</u> is written in "a poor and
probably hasty English hand, with practically no punctuation,"17 and the two extant Heywood manuscripts are only
lightly and somewhat erratically punctuated. If Heywood
expected the first printer of <u>Englands Elizabeth</u> to take
care of the punctuation he picked the wrong man, because
"Beale's punctuation is, for the most part, hopeless."18
Beale's edition would seem to be no improvement over his
copy. Making all of the changes which appear in the second
edition would have been a tedious and lengthy task and it is
difficult to think of Heywood doing it. It is more likely
that he simply relied once again on the printer.

In the matter of actual substantive changes--additions,
deletions, and alterations of words and phrases--in the
second edition, I think Heywood's hand can sometimes be
seen. There is a rather large number of such changes, and
to determine the source of each change two rather difficult
questions must be asked. (1) Could the printer have made
the change; that is, in the normal course of setting type
and trying to follow his copy accurately, is it possible
that the printer accidentally and unconsciously altered the
reading? Some of the variant readings almost certainly
arise in this way; an "s" is omitted and a plural becomes a
singular; a word is skipped ("and" in l. 697) or misread
("happily" for "happly" at l. 2145). (2) Would the printer
have made the change? This is a more difficult question to
answer. It seems that he would have been more likely to
"correct" what he saw as an error in spelling or grammar
than to correct factual errors or to make subtle sophistica-
tions in phrasing. Thus it is quite possible that he

"corrected" Heywood's past participles in lines 682, 718 and 733, changed "weary" to "wearied" (1265), found more common terms for the unusual "assayed" (944) and "apperill" (1400), and corrected the grammar with "impel" (1970). On the other hand, he is not likely to have changed "flye" to "flee" (44) or "February" to "November" (2518). The authority for most of the changes cannot, unfortunately, be assigned with confidence to either Heywood or the printer; more precisely, the two have equal claim to the authority. Beale's poor printing of the first edition produced a large number of blatant errors which either the author or the printer of the second edition would have corrected--there is simply no way to tell who made the corrections.

The third and last of the early editions of Englands Elizabeth was printed in 1641 by Roger Daniel for John Sweeting, Waterhouse presumably having died or otherwise passed on his rights to the book. There is no record in the Stationers' Register of a transfer of the title, and it is not included in the list of Sweeting's titles acquired in 1662 by Robert Horne after Sweeting's death;[19] it was perhaps owned by Daniel.

This edition collates A-I[12] and appears to be simply a reprint of the 1632 edition. It makes a few minor changes which might be attributable to house-styling and a few ("Sostratus" to "Erostratus" at 1. 1858) which suggest editorial intervention, but in virtually all of its readings and its accidentals it agrees with the second edition. There is no evidence that Heywood himself had anything to do with preparing the edition. The exact publication date is not known, but Heywood died in August 1641, at the age of about 67. This is probably the edition listed in the "History" section (sig. X2v) of William London's A Catalogue of the Most Vendible Books in England (1657); the entry reads "Englands Elizabeth, her life and troubles from her minority to the Crown. 12o" and is attributed to Sir John Hayward.[20] Michel Grivelet has suggested that this reprinting was a response to the approaching civil war and the desire among older writers to recall the golden age of Elizabeth.[21]

The copy-text for the present edition is the first edition of 1631; I have used an uncorrected copy--Folger (1)-- and have incorporated the stop-press correction "H. H." at lines 98-99.[22] The copy-text has been collated with the second and third editions and, for the substantives only, the Harleian Miscellany edition.

All emendations of substantives have been recorded in the emendations list. When the reason for emending is not apparent I have tried to clarify it in the Textual Notes.

In general I have tried to be conservative about emendation,
adopting later readings only if they correct a factual error
in 1631[23] or if it seems likely that they could not have
originated with the printer.

I have been more liberal in emending the accidentals.
The first edition may be a fair sample of Heywood's punctuation, but he almost certainly intended the printer to im-
prove it. Beale having failed in the task, it was left to
the printer of the second edition to render the text readable. The changes are necessary if the text is to be made
intelligible; there are long passages of the 1631 edition
with no punctuation except an almost arbitrary scattering of
commas and semicolons, while in other places a comma or
colon appears where a full stop is required.[24] I have made
the decisions about where and how to repunctuate, but because many of my emendations are identical with those made
in the later editions I have followed the practice of
attributing the emendations to these later editions in the
Emendations of Accidentals list.[25]

Several kinds of silent emendations have been made in the
copy-text. Short "s" replaces long "s" and u/v and i/j usage
have been modernized. The ampersand is always expanded to
"and," except where it is used in the abbreviation "&c."
The form "wth" is always expanded to "with." "An." and "Ano"
are expanded to "Anno." The forms "B." and "Bish." have been
expanded to "Bishop"; "S." and "Sr." to "Sir"; "L." to "Lord"
or "Lady" and "Ls." to "Lords" or "Ladies," as appropriate;
and "K." to "King." The abbreviations "Q." and "Qu." have
been expanded and regularized to "Queene," although when the
word is spelled out the copy-text is not always consistent in
maintaining the final "e": "Queen" appears twelve times in
1631 and "Queene" ninety-seven times. "M." and "Master" have
been regularized to "Mr." when they are used as part of a
man's title'; the form "Master" has been retained, of course,
in phrases such as "our King and Master." The copy-text
often follows a numeral with a period; this period has been
silently deleted and appears in the collation only if there
is some other reason to emend the punctuation following a
numeral. 1631 quite often uses the tilde to replace a nasal;
the tilde has been dropped and the nasal inserted. Finally,
turned letters are silently corrected.

The side-notes which appear in all of the early editions
have been eliminated from the present text and are listed
separately; most of them are brief statements of the "action"
at the point at which they appear, but a few of them preserve
valuable information and these are discussed in either the
Textual Notes or the Explanatory Notes.

No effort has been made to preserve either the lineation

or the exact typography of the copy-text although I have retained its italic. Variants arising from a change in type
style alone are not listed. The second and third editions
often replace the italic of 1631 with roman, sometimes of a
larger size; conversely, they occasionally set in italic passages which were roman in the first edition. When it has been
necessary to emend an italicized word in 1631, the italic is
retained regardless of the type style in the source of the
emendation. Thus when readings agree in all respects except
the size and style of type, they are considered to be non-
variant.

A few large decorative initials appear in all of the early editions, usually at the beginning of each major section
of the book; the initial is followed by one or more uppercase
letters. The decorative initial has been silently regularized
to a capital, and the capitals following to lowercase. The
large initial is taken to indicate the beginning of a new
paragraph, and the present edition indents accordingly.

In the emendation tables the reading to the left of the
bracket is from the present text. If an edition (identified
by its siglum: 32 for 1632, 41 for 1641, H for the Harleian
Miscellany reprint) is identified immediately to the right
of the bracket, that is the earliest source of the emendation. It is followed by the reading in the copy-text (1631).
The readings later than that used for the emendation are not
listed, and it cannot be assumed that they agree with the
earliest source of the emendation. The reading of the
earliest emendation is not always exactly as it appears in
the emendation lists. The earliest reading is identified
only for its feature which is relevant to the emendation.
For example, the first emendation note to line 873 is:
Ruines.] 32; ---, 31. This indicates that the full stop
following "Ruines" in the present text is a reading adopted
from the second edition and that it replaces the comma found
in the copy-text. In fact, the reading in 32 is "ruines.";
the present text retains the capitalization from the copy-
text since there is no reason to emend it. Only the salient
feature of the emendation, the punctuation, is noted. If
the bracket is followed immediately by a semicolon, the
emendation has been made by the present editor, and only the
copy-text variant will be listed (unless all later readings
agree with the copy-text, in which case the siglum becomes
31+). A historical collation was compiled for this text but
because of its great length it has been dropped from this
edition. It is available as pp. 193-339 of my dissertation,
"A Critical Old-Spelling Edition of Thomas Heywood's Englands
Elizabeth" (Northern Illinois Univ., 1977).

For typographical convenience, a long dash (---) is used instead of a wavy dash to indicate the repetition of a non-variant word in the emendation notes, and digraphs, in both the text and the notes, are written as two letters.

Notes

1. *A Transcript of the Registers of the Company of Stationers of London*, ed. Edward Arber, IV (1877; rpt. New York: Peter Smith, 1950), 251.

2. Ed. Thomas Park (1813; rpt. New York: AMS, 1965), X, 302-33. Although this is ostensibly a reprint of the 1641 edition, the accidentals are altered to conform to nineteenth-century usage and there are occasional substantive changes.

3. Number 528, The English Experience series (New York: Da Capo, 1973). The copy reproduced is that of the Bodleian (which is in the uncorrected state), with sigs. C1r and C7v from the British Library copy G.1509 and D2r and H1r from the British Library copy 610.a.30.

4. Arthur Brown pointed out the need for "a thorough study of his spelling and his handwriting" more than twenty years ago ("An Edition of the Plays of Thomas Heywood: A Preliminary Survey of Problems," *Renaissance Papers* [1954], p. 75), but nothing definitive or even systematic has been done. Bits and pieces of information are scattered about in a number of sources, as for example: Samuel A. Tannenbaum, *The Handwriting of the Renaissance* (New York: Columbia Univ. Press, 1930); many articles and books relating to the play *Sir Thomas More*, in which "Hand B" is often identified as Heywood's; A. C. Partridge, *Orthography in Shakespeare and Elizabethan Drama* (Lincoln: Univ. of Nebraska Press, 1964), esp. pp. 46-50; Arthur Brown's introduction to the Malone Society edition of *The Captives* (Oxford: Oxford Univ. Press, 1953); and Henry D. Janzen's introduction to the Malone Society edition of *The Escapes of Jupiter* (Oxford: Oxford Univ. Press, 1978).

5. Virtually every editor who has worked with the two plays in the Egerton 1994 manuscript has commented on the handwriting. A. H. Bullen, the first editor of *The Captives*, wrote that the hand was "villainous," "detestable," and "desperately difficult" (*A Collection of Old English Plays* [1885; rpt. New York: Blom, 1964], II, 419; IV, v, 100). In 1925, W. W. Greg ("The Escapes of Jupiter," in *Collected Papers*, ed. J. C. Maxwell [Oxford: Clarendon Press, 1966], pp. 156-83) wrote that "the labour of deciphering the manuscript is considerable" (171); he described the hand as "very difficult" (157, n. 1), "atrocious" (158), and "careless" (162). Arthur Brown, who is currently preparing an edition of all of Heywood's dramatic pieces, wrote that the hand-

writing is "appallingly bad" ("An Edition of the Plays of Thomas Heywood," p. 73). Anthony G. Petti says that "Heywood's hand is probably the least legible of all those extant in Elizabethan dramatic documents" (English Literary Hands from Chaucer to Dryden [London: Edward Arnold, 1977], p. 111).

6. The plays I and II The Fair Maid of the West were also printed in 1631. Part II may have been written as late as 1630, but Part I had probably been written thirty years before; Robert K. Turner, Jr., has found "nothing to show that Heywood provided the text or even reviewed it" although he did give the publisher some dedicatory material (ed., The Fair Maid of the West Parts I and II [Lincoln: Univ. of Nebraska Press, 1967]. p. xix). Turner supposes that because of "the small number of misreading errors, or substantive errors of any sort," the copy from which the printer set was probably not in Heywood's hand (p. xix). In "The Text of Heywood's The Fair Maid of the West," The Library, 5th Ser. 22 (1967), 299–325, Turner makes a sound case for the copy having been a scribal transcription.

7. "The Captives: Foul Papers or Copy?" in The Stability of Shakespeare's Text (Lincoln: Univ. of Nebraska Press, 1965), pp. 200–06.

8. There is a handy, concise sketch of Beale's career in Cyprian Blagden's The Stationers' Company: A History, 1403–1959 (London: Allen & Unwin, 1960), pp. 125–29.

9. C. H. Herford and Percy Simpson, Ben Jonson, I (Oxford: Clarendon Press, 1925), 211. Here and elsewhere, in quotations from manuscript sources, I have expanded the contractions.

10. For a diagram of this format see Philip Gaskell, A New Introduction to Bibliography (Oxford: Clarendon Press, 1972), p. 97 (fig. 55).

11. William Hewer and Henry Holden were almost certainly in Beale's shop. John Dennys was bound to Beale in 1628 and Thomas Ginne in 1625, both for terms of eight years; no record of their date of freedom has survived. Robert Hughes was freed by Beale in 1637, so he was probably apprenticed in 1629 or 1630. See D. F. McKenzie, Stationers' Company Apprentices 1605–1640 (Charlottesville: Bibliographical Society of the Univ. of Virginia, 1961), pp. 9–10.

12. he/hee, she/shee, me/mee, we/wee, be/bee, do/doe, go/goe, been/beene, and Majesty/Majestie.

13. This determination was made using the method described by Kenneth Povey in "The Optical Determination of
First Formes," Studies in Bibliography, 13 (1960), 189-90. I
examined the Newberry copy. The results cannot be accepted
with a high degree of confidence. Povey says that his method
works best with "a crisp, unpressed copy," and that with such
a copy "it is usually possible to recognise the first forme"
(189; my italics). The Newberry copy is a far remove from
"crisp, unpressed." Hinman's technique of tracing the re-
appearance of distinctive pieces of type may have been helpful but so much of Beale's type is either broken or poorly
inked that I have been unable to identify distinct pieces with
certainty. I have not tried Sullivan's method of checking
for recurring rules; see Ernest W. Sullivan, II, "Marginal
Rules as Evidence," Studies in Bibliography, 30 (1977),
171-80.

14. Henry R. Plomer, A Dictionary of the Booksellers and
Printers Who Were at Work in England, Scotland and Ireland
from 1641 to 1667 (London: The Bibliographical Society, 1907),
p. 60.

15. After 1603, according to McKerrow, the modern use of
i and j and of capitals "seems to have spread more and more,
though it was not until about 1630 that it became the normal
one. A reprint of an earlier work published after that date
will generally substitute the modern usage for the old,
though there are still exceptions" (Ronald B. McKerrow, "Some
Notes on the Letters i, j, u and v in Sixteenth Century Printing," The Library, 3rd Ser., 1 [1910], 257). McKerrow gives
Heywood's Pleasant Dialogues and Drammas (1637) as an example
of a work in which both conventions appear. David M. Bergeron
("Two Compositors in Heywood's Londons Ius Honorarium (1631),"
Studies in Bibliography, 22 [1969], 223-26) found that the
mixture of u/v usage in Heywood's first Lord Mayor's pageant
was the result of differing compositorial practice.

16. Such a practice is not unknown, however. R. H.
Miller has shown that Sir John Harington made just such
changes in his holograph manuscript of A Supplie or Addicion
to the Catalogue of Bishops, to the yeare 1608: "contrary to
traditional assumptions about spelling practices of the
period, Harington consciously altered his own spelling patterns from one manuscript to the other. . . . The alterations themselves show generally that Harington attempted to
'modernize' and regularize spelling . . ." ("Early Seventeenth-Century Spelling Patterns: Two Autograph Manuscripts
by Sir John Harington," a paper delivered at the Third Saint

xxxvi

Louis Conference on Manuscript Studies, Saint Louis University, 14-16 October 1976; the quotations are from an abstract
which appeared in Manuscripta, 21 [1977], 19-20). Harington
was working under special circumstances--preparing a presentation copy for the Prince of Wales--which Heywood was not, but
Miller is right to point out the danger of assuming that an
author's spelling habits are somehow genetically acquired and
thus cannot change.

17. Partridge, p. 170.

18. Herford and Simpson, VI, 150.

19. George E. B. Eyre, ed., A Transcript of the Registers
of the Worshipful Company of Stationers; from 1640-1708, II
(1913; rpt. Gloucester, Mass.: Peter Smith, 1967), 313-14.
There is no mention of Englands Elizabeth in the Register
during these years; I am grateful to Professor William P.
Williams for allowing me to consult an early typescript of
his Index to the Stationers' Register 1640-1708 (LaJolla,
Calif.: Laurence McGilvery, 1980).

20. Facsimile rpt. London: Gregg, 1965. Series 2, no. 2,
English Bibliographical Sources, ed. D. F. Foxon. London's
confusion over the name arose from the error in the previous
entry, Hayward's Life and Reign of King Edward the Sixth,
where the author is named "Jo. Haywood." For Englands Elizabeth a dash is substituted for the author's name. London provides little helpful information except to say that "such
[books] as I mention, are to my own knowledg usually sold in
most places of repute in the Country, and is fully useful to
the private end I first intended by this Catalogue, viz. the
use of the Northern Counties" (sig. Clr).

21. Thomas Heywood et le drame domestique élizabéthain
(Paris: Didier, 1957), pp. 86-87.

22. "A bibliographical editor should not slavishly follow a press-corrected reading until he has determined, first,
that the uncorrected typesetting was indeed corrupt; and,
second, if so, that he cannot better emend on the evidence
furnished by the corruption before he accepts into his text
what in the majority of cases is no more than an unauthoritative guess or rationalization of the printing-house reader.
These press-variants and their customary editorial treatment
are instances of the fact that a little bibliography can be a
dangerous thing"; Fredson Bowers, On Editing Shakespeare and
the Elizabethan Dramatists (Philadelphia: Univ. of Pennsyl-

vania Library, 1955), p. 49. A thorough examination of Heywood's relationship with his printers is needed. He several
times complains in prefaces about careless printers and about
his plays having been printed without his knowledge. However,
in "A Proof-sheet in Thomas Heywood's The Iron Age," The
Library, 5th Ser., 10 (1955), Arthur Brown has found that although the play was extensively corrected while being printed, "there is little to support the possibility that Heywood
himself had anything to do with it" (278).

    23. A large number of factual errors remain. To correct
these in the text would, in some cases (ll. 791-95, for example), have been impossible, but they are corrected in the
Explanatory Notes. The errors are not likely to cause a
problem since no modern historian is apt to go to Englands
Elizabeth for reliable information about Elizabeth's early
life. The errors are also retained, of course, because they
appear to be authorial and they may have some positive value
in providing clues to Heywood's sources or to his understanding of the period about which he is writing.

    24. In preparing his Malone Society edition of The
Escapes of Jupiter, Janzen found that "the punctuation of the
text is rather haphazard and no clear principles are apparent.
Periods are frequently found in the middle of a sentence . . .
(p. viii).

    25. Bowers summarizes the commonly received opinion on
this matter: "Every critical editor finds it convenient to
synthesize his copy-text with various readings from . . .
unauthoritative editions; and Shakespeare's received text is
sprinkled with good guesses, and some not so good, from the
Second, Third, and Fourth Folios. In each case, however, if
the editor is operating according to right principles, he
elects these readings not because they can have any possible
authority, but because their guesses coincide with the readings that he would himself have made independently" (On Editing Shakespeare, p. 77).

ENGLANDS

ELIZABETH:

HER LIFE AND

TROUBLES,

During Her Minoritie,

from the Cradle to the

CROWNE.

TO THE RIGHT HONOURABLE the Lord HENRY <u>Earle</u>

of <u>Dover</u>, <u>Viscount</u> ROCHFORD, L. <u>Hunsdon</u>, <u>&c</u>.

<u>Right</u> <u>Honourable</u>,

When I had finished this short Tractate (which

may bee rather styl'd a superficiall remembrance then

an essentiall expression of the passages of Queene

<u>Elizabeth's</u> Life in her minoritie), I could not

apprehend unto whom the Patronage thereof might more

justly belong, then to your Honour, whose noble

Grandfather, <u>Henry</u> Lord <u>Hunsdon</u>, after Lord   10

<u>Chamberlaine</u> to her Majestie (her neere and deare

Kinsman) was the most constant Friend and faithfull

Assistant in all her troubles and dangers, who not

onely imploy'd his whole industry, and made Use of

his best Friends, but liberally expended his means,

and hazarded his owne person as an Interposer betwixt

her safety and the malice of her both cruell and

potent adversaries. Which makes me somthing to

wonder, that so great and remarkeable a zeale exprest

in a time of such inevitable danger, when all Her   20

friends were held the Queene her Sisters enemies, and

her enemies, the Queenes friends; when nothing but

Examinations, sentences of Imprisonment, and terrours

of Death were thundred against her; that he (I say)
whom neither promises of favor could disswade from
her Love, nor threatnings of death, deterre from her
Service, should not bee so much as once remembred by
the Collectors of Her History.

Be this therefore (Right Honourable) a lasting
Testimony of his unchanged affection to her and her   30
Innocence from the beginning, as likewise, a long-
liv'd Monument of her Royall gratitude towards him,
extended even unto his end, and to his noble Issue
after him. What great confidence shee had in his
loyalty appeared at the Campe of Tilbury in the yeare
1588, where hee solely commanded the Guard for her
Majesties owne Person, which consisted of Lances,
Light-Horse, and Foote, to the number of 34050.

It hath pleased your Lordship to censure
favourably of some of my weak Labours not long since   40
presented before you, which the rather encouraged mee
to make a free tender of this small peece of service.
In which if my boldnesse should beget the least
distast from you, I must flee for refuge to those
words of the Poet Claudian.

----- ----- - Leones, Quae stravisse valent,
ea mox prostrata relinquunt.

Thus wishing to you and to all your Noble
Family, not onely the long fruition of the blessings
of this life present, but the eternall possession of   50
the Joyes future, I remaine your Lordships,

In all observances;

THOMAS HEYVVOOD.

TO THE GENEROUS READER.

Were I able to write this little Historicall
Tractate with the Pen of Tacitus, the Inke of
Curtius, and set downe every line and letter by
Epictetus his Candle, yet can I see no possibilitie
to avoyd the Criticks of this age, who with their
frivolous cavils and unnecessary exceptions, ambush   60
the commendable labours of others, when they
themselves will not or dare not either through
idlenesse or ignorance, adventure the expence of one
serious hower in any laborious worke intended for the
benefit of either Church or Common-weale; and such
Polypragmatists this age is full of;
        --Sed meliora spero,

    I doubt not but that they will spare this
Argument for the worth thereof, and though their
carping may correct my Poeme, yet they will have a   70
reverend respect of the Person here drawne out, whose
never-dying fame even in this our age is so sacred
amongst all good men, that it is scarce remembred, at
the least uttered without a devout thanks-giving.

    The prosperous and successfull Reigne of this
Royall Queene and Virgin hath been largely delivered

in the Latine Tongue whereby all forraigne Nations have beene made partakers of her admirable vertues and religious Government; but for that part of her Life, during her tender and sappy Age, all our domesticke remembrancers have beene sparing to speake.

As they have shewed you a Queene, I expose to your view a Princesse; they in her Majestie, I in her Minority; they the passages of her incomparable Life from the Scepter to the Sepulchre, as shee was a Soveraigne; I the processe of her time from the Cradle to the Crowne, as she was a sad and sorrowfull Subject; in the discovery whereof, I have not fallen so pat as to make the relation of her Minority the whole scope of my intentions, but have for the better enlightening thereof, made use of all such eminent occurrences of State, as may aptly introduce thereunto. As for those passages in the Characterizing of King Edward the sixth, and the Lady Jane Gray, and others;

                    --vix ea nostra voco,

I have borrowed them from my good friend Mr. H. H. Stationer, who hath not onely conversed with the titles of Bookes, but hath looked into them, and from

80

90

100

8

thence drawne out that industrious Collection,

Intituled Herologia Anglicana. Not to hold thee any

longer in that to which all this but introduceth. If

the Booke please thee, I am satisfied, and shall rest

still,

Thine;

N. R.

ENGLANDS ELIZABETH. Her LIFE, and TROUBLES.

The better to illustrate this history, needfull
it is that wee speak somthing of the Mother, before   110
we proceed to the Daughter.

A match was concluded betwixt Prince Arthur the
eldest Sonne and Heyre apparant to Henry the 7th,
King of England, and the Infant Katharine daughtter
to the King of Spaine. Shee landed at Plymouth Anno
1501 and was married to Prince Arthur; in Aprill next
following hee expired at Ludlow, in that Castle,
which hath beene an ancient Seate belonging to the
Princes of Wales. Death having thus made a Divorce
betwixt these two Princes, the two mighty and potent   120
Kings (by their grave and politick governments knowne
to bee as eminent in wisdome as greatnesse), for the
more assured continuance of league and amity betwixt
them, treated of a second match betwixt Henry the
second sonne (but then the Sole Heyre and hope of
England) and the late Dowager, Princesse of Spaine.
The contract by a dispensation solicited, and after
granted by the pope then raigning was accordingly
performed. The marriage countenanced by their knowne
wisdomes on the one side, and authorized by his   130

Ecclesiasticall Jurisdiction on the other side, was held not onely tolerable but irrevocable.

Notwithstanding, the Father dying, and the Soveraigne Sonne inaugurated by the name of <u>Henry</u> the eight, for many yeeres together enjoying a peaceable and quiet raigne, whether distasting his Queene, by reason that by this time she was growne somewhat in yeeres, or that hee had cast an affectionate eye upon a more choice beauty, or that through scruple of Conscience (which for his honors sake is most received) I am not able to censure. But sure it is, that hee beganne deepely to consider with himselfe, that notwithstanding the usurped liberty of the <u>Pope</u> (whose Prerogative till then was never thought disputable) that his marriage was not onely unlawfull, but incestuous. Some are of opinion that hee was hereunto moved by the Nobility; others, that hee was instigated by the Clergy. But if we may give credit to his owne Protestation in open Court, the first original of this touch in Conscience was because the Bishop of <u>Bayon</u>, being sent Ambassador from the <u>French</u> King to debate a Marriage betwixt the Duke of <u>Orleance</u> his second sonne, and the Lady <u>Mary</u>, the sole surviving Issue of him and his Queene

140

150

Katharine, as the match was upon the point to bee
concluded, the Bishop beganne to demurre and desired
respit, till he were fully resolved whether the Lady
Mary (by reason of the Kings Marriage with his
brothers wife) were legitimate or not. The cause is
doubtfull, but the effect I am sure is   160
unquestionable.

    Although the King received from this Spanish Lady
a Prince called Henry, borne at Richmond on Newyeeres
day in the second yeer of his raigne, for whose
Nativity great Triumphs were kept at Westminster, yet
breathed his last upon Saint Mathews day following.
Besides hee had by her a second issue, the Lady Mary
before-named, so that neither sterility and
barrennesse could be aspersed upon her, nor any
knowne disobedience or disloyalty objected against   170
her, but that (as the King himselfe often protested)
she was a wife no way refractory, but in all things
corresponding to his desires and pleasures. These
things notwithstanding, the pretended divorce was, to
the Kings great cost and charge, so effectually
negotiated, that after they had lived together by the
space of 22 yeeres and upwards in unquestioned
Matrimony, it was made the publique Argument in

Schooles, debated by the <u>Italian</u>, <u>French</u>, <u>German</u>, and
our owne moderne Doctors, both Ecclesiasticall and   180
Civill, by an unanimous consent determined, and for
the better confirmation thereof, by the Seales of
divers Academies signed, that the Marriage betwixt
the King and Queene (never till now called his
Sister, or Brothers wife) was a meere nullity,
absolutely unlawfull, and that his sacred Majesty had
liberty and licence (howsoever the <u>Pope</u> sought by all
meanes to antipose their opinions) warrantable from
them, after a legal divorce sued out from the Court,
to make choice of any other lady to his wife where he   190
himselfe best liked.

Cardinall <u>Campeius</u> was sent from his Holinesse
and Cardinall <u>Wolsey</u> was joyned with him in
commission, to determine of this difficult point.
The King and Queene were convened in open Court, then
held in <u>Black Friers</u>. The Resolution of the weighty
Argument then in hand was so abstruse, that it puzled
all; though many seemed confident, yet not a few of
the best Orthodoxall divines then staggered in their
opinions, in so much that the Legate departed the   200
land before he would give up a definitive sentence in
the cause: the reason was because hee desired further

Order and Instruction from his Holinesse.

In the Interim the good Princess, greatly beloved, was much pittied, and the King, much honored, was greatly feared. (For now most mens thoughts were in their hearts, a time better to thinke then speake.) But before the Divorce was publikly denounced, the Lady <u>Anne</u> <u>Bullein</u> on the first of <u>September</u> <u>Anno</u> 1532, was at <u>Windsor</u> created 210 Marchiones of <u>Pembrooke</u>, and one thousand pound <u>per</u> <u>annum</u> conferred upon her by the King, which news no sooner arrived to the dejected Princesse eare, but shee beganne to consider with her selfe the ficklenesse and instability of greatnesse; and seeing that Sunne to set in a cloud on her, which was beginning to rise serenely on another, who was now majestically ascending those steps by which shee was miserably descending, exprest a womans wondrous modesty, and without speaking any distastfull or 220 irreverent word against the King, said: <u>Great</u> <u>men</u> <u>enterprizing</u> <u>great</u> <u>things</u>, <u>ought</u> <u>neither</u> <u>by</u> <u>the</u> <u>Lawes</u> <u>of</u> <u>God</u> <u>nor</u> <u>man</u> <u>to</u> <u>employ</u> <u>their</u> <u>power</u> <u>as</u> <u>their</u> <u>owne</u> <u>mind</u> <u>willeth</u>, <u>but</u> <u>as</u> <u>Justice</u> <u>and</u> <u>Reason</u> <u>teacheth</u>: but fearing lest in speaking so little she had spoken too much, shut up the rest of what shee thought to utter, in a modest and welbeseeming silence.

Upon the 25 of <u>January</u> <u>Anno</u> 1533, the King was
married in his Closset at <u>Whitehall</u>, to the
Marchionesse of <u>Pembrooke</u>, the Lady, <u>Anne</u> <u>Bullein</u>,   230
but very privately: few were present at the
ceremonies, then celebrated by Dr. <u>Rowland</u> <u>Lee</u>, not
long after consecrated Bishop of <u>Chester</u>.

In this concealed Solemnity, one Mistresse <u>Anne</u>
<u>Savage</u>, much trusted by them both, bore up the
Queenes traine. This Lady was within few moneths
after espoused to the Lord <u>Berkely</u>.

In <u>Easter</u> <u>Eve</u> being the 12 of <u>Aprill</u>, the Queene
being known to the King to bee young with child, went
to the Chappell openly as a Queene, and was   240
proclaimed publikly the same day Queene of <u>England</u>
and upon <u>Whitsunday</u> following crowned at <u>Westminster</u>,
with all the pompe, state and magnificence therto
belonging. Queene <u>Katharine</u>, who for many yeeres had
been their Soveraigne Lady, is now quite forgotten,
and Queene <u>Anne</u>, being to the people scarcely known,
is soly honored. The rising Sunne is onely adored:
their joyful acclamations readier for the coronation
of the one, then their unjust exclamations to forward
the deposing of the other.   250

Upon the 7th of <u>September</u>, being <u>Sunday</u>, betwixt
the houres of 3 and 4 in the Afternoone, Queene <u>Anne</u>
was delivered of a fayre daughter at <u>Greenewich</u>, who,
to the great unspeakable joy, both of Prince and
people, was christened on the third day following
being <u>Wednesday</u>; the Mayor of <u>London</u> and his
brethren, with more then forty other of the gravest
Citizens, being commanded to attend upon the
solemnities. It was performed in the Fryers Church
in <u>Greenewich</u>. The Font was of silver, placed in the   260
middle of the church with an ascent of three steps
high; the old Dutchesse of <u>Norfolke</u> bore the Babe
wrap'd in a Mantle of purple velvet. The Consponsors
or witnesses were <u>Thomas</u> <u>Cranmer</u>, Arch-bishop of
<u>Canterbury</u>, the Dutchesse of <u>Norfolke</u>, and the
Marchionesse of <u>Dorset</u>, both widdowes.

Not long after the birth of the Lady <u>Elizabeth</u>, a
generall oath of allegiance past thorow the kingdom,
to bind al such as by their yeers were capable
thereof, to maintaine and uphold the successive   270
heyres descending from the bodies of the King and
Queen <u>Anne</u>, lawfully begotten in the true and legall
possession of the Throne, Crown, Sword and Scepter,
with all the royalties and imperiall honors thereunto

belonging.

The conjecturall of the administration of this
oath, together with the suddenesse of the Queenes
coronation, was to strenthen the match, and make the
legitimation of her issue (which by the Kings former
match was amongst many yet made questionable) of more   280
validity: for (as one observeth) Anna coronatur, quod
nulli nisi regni haeredibus contingere solet: Queene
Anne was therefore crowned, because it is an honour
soly conferred upon such whose issue are capable of
succession. Wherby it is probable that the Kings
purpose was to adnihilate and extinguish the Title of
his daughter Mary, and to leave the Crowne and
dignity Royall to the sole heires of Queene Anne.
For this cause were the two young Ladies brought up
apart, which may be a reason why they were after so   290
different in their dispositions, and so opposite in
their Religions: both of them, though not sucking the
milke, yet as well imitating the mindes as following
the steps of their mothers; Queene Katharine living
and dying a constant Romane Catholique; Queene Anne,
both in her life and death, resolute in the defence
of the Reformed Religion, which (as the most probable
conjectures have left to us upon file) was, by the

instigation of some Romists then powerfull with the
King, who was not then fully setled in those tenents   300
which he after made his maxims, the prologue to her
fall and lives Catastrophe which not long after
hapned.

On Mayday, Anno 1536, was a great justing held at
Greenewich, in the which the chiefe challenger was
the Lord Rochford, brother to the Queene, and the
defendants were one Henry Norrice of the Kings
Bedchamber, with others. They mannaged their armes
with great dexterity, and every course which they
ranne came off with the lowd applause of the people,   310
insomuch that the King at first sight seemed in
outward shewe to be wonderously delighted; but about
the middle of the triumph, like a storme in the midst
of a quiet Sea, the King arose suddenly from his
seat, and attended with 6 persons only, tooke Barge,
and was row'd to Westminster, leaving no small
amazement behinde him, every one wondring and
conjecturing as their affections led them, what might
be the occasion thereof. All things were with the
night husht up and in quiet, no appearance of   320
discontent eyther in King or Courtier perceived; but
no sooner did the day peep out, but the King's

discontent appeared with it. George Bulleine, Lord
Rochford the Queenes brother, and Henry Norrice, the
defendant, were saluted with a cold breakfast next
their hearts in their beds, and both conveyed to the
Tower; the newes being brought to the Queene, struck
as cold to her heart, and having past over dinner
with discontent, because the King, as his custome
was, had sent none of his waiters to bid Much good   330
doe it her, at the Table, but perceiving her servants
about her, some with their eyes glazed in teares, but
all with looks dejected on the earth, it bred strange
conceptions in her, yet being confident in her own
innocency, bred in her rather amazement then feare.

The same day entred into her chamber, Sir Thomas
Audley, Lord Chancellor, the Duke of Norfolke, Thomas
Cromwell, Secretary, and at a distance after them,
Sir William Kinsman, Constable of the Tower. At
their first appearance, her apprehension was that   340
they were sent from the King to comfort her about the
imprisonment of her brother; but observing them to
looke more austerely upon her, then usually they were
accustomed, shee began to mistrust their message.
But casting her eye beyond them, and espying the
Constable of the Tower to accompany them in their

unwelcome visit, she grew then confident that her
death was now approaching, and that these were the
Heralds to prepare it; so expressing more modesty
then Majesty, both in her behaviour and countenance, 350
she prepared her selfe to attend their message, which
the Chancellor delivered unto her in few words,
telling her that it was his Majesties command that
she must instantly be conveyed from thence to the
Tower, there to remaine during his highnes pleasure.
To which she answered that her innocence and patience
had armed her against all adversities whatsoever, and
if such were his Majesties command and pleasure, they
both should with all humility be obeyed. So without
change of habit, or any thing necessary for her 360
remoove, shee put her selfe into their safe custody,
and by them was conveyed into her Barge.

Just upon the stroke of five, she entred the
Tower. The Lords with the Lieutenant, brought her to
her Chamber, to whome, at their departure, she spoke
these few words following (falling upon her knees.) I
beseech God Almighty to be my assistance and helpe,
onely so farre forth as I am not guiltie of any just
crime that may be layd against me. Then turning to
the Lords, I intreat you to beseech the King in my 370

behalfe, that it will please him to be a good Lord
unto mee; which words were no sooner uttered, but
they departed.

The fifteenth of the same moneth, the Lords of
the Councell met at the Tower. The Queene was called
to the Barre, and arraigned before the Duke of
Norfolk, who sate as Lord high Steward, the Lord
Chancellor on the right hand, and the Duke of
Suffolke on the left hand, with divers others
Marquesses, Earles, and Barons; the Earle of Surrey,   380
sonne to the Duke of Norfolke, sate directly before
his father, a degree lower, as Earle Marshall of
England. The Queene sitting in a chaire, divers
accusations, especially touching inconstancy, were
objected against her, to all which she answered
punctually with such gravity and discretion that it
appeared to her Auditory she could not bee found
guilty of any aspersion whatsoever. But when in
their favourable censures they were readye (not
without great applause) to acquit her, the Jury   390
brought in a contrary verdict, by which shee was
convicted, condemned, and had her judgement to be
burned, or else her head to be cut off at the Kings
pleasure. The Sentence being denounced, the Court

arose, and she was conveyed backe againe to her
Chamber, the <u>Lady</u> <u>Bullein</u> her Aunt and the <u>Lady</u>
<u>Kinsman</u>, wife to the Constable of the <u>Tower</u>, onely
attending her.

Two dayes after were brought unto the <u>Tower-Hill</u>
<u>George</u> <u>Lord</u> <u>Rochford</u>, <u>Henry</u> <u>Norris</u>, <u>Marke</u> <u>Smeton</u>,   400
<u>William</u> <u>Brierton</u>, <u>Francis</u> <u>Weston</u>, all of them of the
Kings Privy Chamber, who severally suffered and had
their heads stricken off, no other account of their
sufferings being given out abroad, but that they
deservedly dyed for matters concerning the convicted
Queene.

Two dayes after, the Queene was brought to the
<u>greene</u> within the <u>Tower</u>, and there mounted on a
Scaffold where were present most part of the
Nobility, the <u>Lord</u> <u>Mayor</u> of <u>London</u>, with certaine   410
<u>Aldermen</u> and many other Spectators. Her last words
were these: <u>My</u> <u>honourable</u> <u>Lords</u>, <u>and</u> <u>the</u> <u>rest</u> <u>here</u>
<u>assembled</u>, <u>I</u> <u>beseech</u> <u>you</u> <u>all</u> <u>to</u> <u>beare</u> <u>witnesse</u> <u>with</u>
<u>me</u> <u>that</u> <u>I</u> <u>humbly</u> <u>submit</u> <u>my</u> <u>selfe</u> <u>to</u> <u>undergoe</u> <u>the</u>
<u>penalty</u> <u>to</u> <u>which</u> <u>the</u> <u>Law</u> <u>hath</u> <u>sentenced</u> <u>me</u>. <u>As</u>
<u>touching</u> <u>my</u> <u>offences</u>, <u>I</u> <u>am</u> <u>sparing</u> <u>to</u> <u>speak</u>; <u>they</u> <u>are</u>
<u>best</u> <u>knowne</u> <u>to</u> <u>God</u>, <u>and</u> <u>I</u> <u>neither</u> <u>blame</u> <u>nor</u> <u>accuse</u>
<u>any</u> <u>man</u>, <u>but</u> <u>commit</u> <u>them</u> <u>wholly</u> <u>to</u> <u>him</u>, <u>beseeching</u>

God that knowes the secrets of all hearts to have
mercy on my Soule. Next I beseech the Lord Jesus to   420
blesse and save my Soveraigne and Master the King,
the noblest and mercifullest Prince that lives, whom
I wish long to reigne over you. He hath made me
Marchionesse of Pembrooke, vouchsafed me to lodge in
his owne bosome; higher on earth hee could not raise
me, and hath done therefore well to lift me up to
those blessed Innocents in Heaven. Which having
uttered with a smiling and cheerefull countenance, as
no way frighted with the Terrour of Death, She gently
submitted her selfe to her fate, and kneeling down on   430
both her knees, with this short ejaculation in her
mouth, Lord Jesus Christ, into thy hands I commend my
Soule, with the close of the last syllable the
Hangman of Callis at one blow struck off her head.

Phoenix Anna iacet,

nato Phoenice, dolendum,

Saecula Phoenices nulla

tulisse duos.

The King loth to shew himselfe too sad a widdower
for so good a wife, the very next ensuing day was   440
married to the Lady Jane Seymor, daughter to Sir John
Seymor Knight, Sister to Edward Seymor Earle of

Hertford, and Duke of Somerset.

Queene Anne was no sooner frowned on by the King,
but she was abandoned by her late friends and
servants. The young Lady her Daughter lost a Mother
before she could doe any more but smile upon her.
She dyed the Phoenix of her Sexe, but left a daughter
behind who proved the Phoenix of her time, the true
Daughter of so rare a Mother Phoenix. Queene Jane is   450
now the sole object of all the Peoples joy, but
within little more then the Revolution of one yeare
all their hopes are crossed; death nip't the bud but
preserved the blossome for awhile after.

On the 12 day of October in the yeare 1537 the
Queene was delivered both of a Son and her own life
together at Hampton Court about two of the clocke in
the afternoone. It is said, that newes being brought
to the King in the time of her travell, that her
throwes were very violent, insomuch that her life was   460
in great perill by reason of the extremities of her
hard labour, nay that the issue was driven to so
strait an exigent, that either the mother or the
infant must necessarily perish; humbly desiring his
Highnesse in so great extremity; his answer was that
the Mother then should die, for certaine hee was that

hee could have more wives, but uncertaine whether to
have more children. Heereupon preparation was made
to save both, if possible, but her body was ripped up
to give way to her Child in the conclusion, and two   470
dayes after her delivery her Soule expired.

The Queene dyed much pittyed, and the young
Prince called <u>Edward</u> was the eighteenth of the same
moneth created Prince of <u>Wales</u>, Duke of <u>Cornewall</u> and
<u>Chester</u>.

The Father was so joyfull of his Sonne that hee
seemed to cast a neglect upon his two daughters; yet
of them both, the Lady <u>Elizabeth</u> was in most favor
and grace, for when <u>Mary</u> was separated from the
Court, and not so much as suffered to come within a   480
certain distance thereof limited, the Lady <u>Elizabeth</u>
was then admitted to keepe the young Prince company
in his infancy, who in the time of his minority was
committed to the tuition of Doctor <u>Coxe</u> and Sir <u>John</u>
<u>Cheeke</u>. As they were guardians and Schoole-masters
to the Prince, so were they the dayly Instructors of
the sweet young Lady. Shee was 3 yeares elder then
her Brother, and therefore able in her pretty
language to teach and direct him (even from the first
of his speech and understanding) in the principles of   490

Religion and other Documents. The Arch-bishop
Cranmer her God-father was ever chary and tender over
her, as one that at the Font had tooke charge upon
him to see her educated in all vertue and piety.
Cordiall and intire grew the affection betwixt this
brother and Sister, insomuch that he no sooner began
to know her, but hee seemed to acknowledge her, and
she being of more maturity as deeply loved him. Both
comming out of one loynes, their affection was no
lesse then if they had issued likewise from one   500
wombe. They were indeede one way equally fortunate
and unfortunate, having one Father, and either of
them deprived of a Mother, and even in their severall
deaths there was a kind of correspondencie: the one
dyed by the sword, the other in Child-bed, both of
them violent and enforced deaths.

So pregnant and ingenious were either, that they
desired to looke upon bookes as soone as the day
began to breake. Their horae matutinae were so
welcome, that they seemed to prevent the nights   510
sleeping for the entertainment of the morrows
schooling. Besides, such were the hopefull
inclinations of this Princely youth and pious Virgin,
that their first houres were spent in Prayers and

other Religious exercises, as either reading some
History or other in the Old Testament, or else
attending the exposition of some Text or other in the
New; the rest of the fore-noone (Breakfast-time
excepted) they were doctrinated and instructed either
in language, or some of the liberal Sciences, one   520
morrall learning or other collected out of such
Authors as did best conduce to the Instruction of
Princes. And when hee was cal'd out to any youthfull
exercise becomming a Child of his age (for study
without action breedes dulnesse) she in her private
Chamber betooke her selfe to her Lute or violl, and
(wearyed with that) to practise her needle. This was
the circular course of their employment. God was the
Center of all their actions. _Ab_ _Jove_ _Principium_: they
began with God, and hee went along still with them;   530
insomuch that in a short time they were as well
entered into languages as Arts. Most of the frequent
tongues of Christendom they now made theirs. _Greeke_,
Latine, _French_, _Italian_, _Spanish_, _Dutch_ were no
strangers, no forraigne Idiomes, but now made
familiar with their native English,

       -------_Merito_ _ut_ _puer_

           unicus _orbis_

Iure vocaretur Phoenix:

virgo altera Pallas.   540

These concurrences met in such a Concordancie
that the Schollers (though Princes) for their good
instructions were in a kind of duty obliged to their
Tutors; and their Tutors (for their willingnesse and
Industry) as much grac'd and honour'd by their
Schollers. Alexander the great confessed himselfe
more obliged to Aristotle his Schoole-master for his
learning, then to his Father King Philip for his
life; by the one he became a Man, by the other an
understanding Man. This Princely couple cannot bee   550
taxed of ingratitude; if all the malice in the world
were infused into one eye, it shall never be able to
detract either of them. How forward was the one
during his time to promote Doctor Coxe his Tutor, and
the life of that Marian persecution being drawn to
the last breath, the other recald him from beyond the
Seas, whither he was fled, restor'd him to many
Church dignities and grac'd him so far as that by her
appointment he made a learned Sermon that day when
she went to her first Parliament.   560

These tender young Plants being past their sappy
age, and now beginning to flourish, the old stocke

begins to wither. The King feeling himself
dangerously sick, many infirmities growing more and
more upon him, cal'd his Councell about him, made his
last will and Testament, part of which, so much as
concernes this present Discourse, shall be delivered
as it hath been extracted out of the originall
Coppie, still reserved in the Treasury of the
Exchequer, Dated the Thirtieth day of December 1546.   570
Item, I give and bequeath unto our two Daughters,
Mary and Elizabeth, if they shall be marryed to any
outward Potentates, the Summe of tenn-Thousand pounds
a peecee, and that to be paid them by the consent of
our Councell, in Money, Plate, Jewels and Houshold-
stuffe, if wee bestow them not in our life time, or a
larger Summe at the discretion of our Executors, or
the most part of them. And both of them upon our
blessing to be ordered aswell in marriage, as all
other lawfull things, by the advice of our fore-said   580
Councell, and in case they will not, that then those
Summes are to be diminished at our Councels pleasure.
Further, our will is, that from the first houre of
our death, untill such time as they can provide
either of them, or both, of an honourable Marriage,
they shall have either of them, or both of them,

three Thousand pounds ultra Reprisas to live upon. I
have knowne many a Noble Man's Daughter left as great
a Legacie, nay a larger Dower, who never had any
claime or alliance to a Crowne; but so it pleased the   590
King at that time.

Upon the nineteenth day of January following the
King, lying upon his death-bed, even when hee was
ready to give an accompt to God for the aboundance of
bloud already spilt, when hee knew himselfe was no
longer able to live, hee imprisoned the Duke of
Norfolke the Father, signed a warrant for the
execution of the Earle of Surrey, the Sonne; within
nine dayes after he himselfe expired and on the
eighteenth of February following was with great State   600
and magnificence interred at Windsore.

On the same day wherin the Father deceased was
the Sonne inaugurated King of England by the name of
Edward the sixth being of the age of 9 yeares. On
the nineteenth of February following he rode with his
Uncle the Lord Protector, Duke of Sommerset, through
the Citie of London, and the next day ensuing was
anoynted King at West-minster by Thomas Cranmer
Archbishop of Canterbury who that day administred the
holy Eucharist together with sundry other Ceremonies   610

appropriated for such Solemnities.

Great is the person of a King; reigning heere
upon earth amongst men, hee is a lively Embleme of
the high and glorious Majesty of God in heaven. The
King was no sooner crowned, but the Lady <u>Elizabeth</u>
gave way to his State. There was now a
discontinuance of that frequent and private
familiarity usuall betwixt them; formerly she loved
him as a Brother, now she honours him as her
Soveraigne. Honour and Royalty make difference   620
betwixt the Sonne and the Father, the degrees of
State distinguish betwixt brother and Sister; they
which lived sociably in all familiarity together, now
doe not so much as talke but at a distance. The
death of the Father which raysed him to the Crowne,
removed her from the Court, set him in the Throne,
sent her downe into the Countrey; in which retirement
being nobly attended as well by divers voluntary
Ladies and Gentle-women as her owne traine and
houshould Servants, she led there, though a more   630
solitary yet a much more contented life, as having
now more leisure houres to contemplate and ruminate
on those Rudiments and Exercises wherein she had
formerly beene conversant. Diligence is the breeder

and productor of Arts; but practise and exercise doth
nourish and cherish them. She in her great
discretion made gainfull use of this Solitude, as is
apparant by the future.

Being setled in the Country, to adde unto her
Revenue, shee had many gifts and visits sent her from
the King, who was very carefull both of her honour
and health. Shee lived under the charge of a noble
and vertuous Lady, who was stil'd her Governesse.
Scarce was she yet full fourteene yeares of age when
one of her Uncles, then in great office and place
about the King, brought unto her a Princely Suitor,
as great in means as comely in Person. A stranger
richly habited and nobly attended, (whose name my
Author gives not!) he, after much importunitie both
from himselfe and friends, yet at last crost in his
purpose by modest repulses and cold answeres, and
finding her immutable disposition solely addicted to
a single life, as not enduring the name of a husband,
setled in his mind (though not satisfied in her
denyall) retyred into his Countrey. For though it
may be said of women in generall, that they are spare
in their answeres, and peremptory in their demands
and purposes, that their affections are stil in the

640

650

extreames, either so passionate as by no counsell to
be redressed, or so counterfeit, as to be by no man   660
beleeved, and again, if they are beautiful they are
to be won with prayses, if coy with prayers, if proud
with gifts, and if covetous with promises; yet this
sweet Lady, tho her beauty were attractive, yet by no
flattery could be removed from her setled resolution,
and being conscious neither of Pride, coyness, or
covetousnes, could not be easily drawn within the
compas of any subtile temptation. This first
unwelcome motion of Marriage was a cause why shee
lived afterwards more solitary and retyred. If at   670
any time the King her Brother upon any weighty or
important occasion had sent to enjoy her company at
Court, she made no longer Residence then to know his
highnesse pleasure and to make humble tender of her
duty and allegiance. That done, with all convenient
speed she returned backe into the Country, where she
spent the entire season of her Brothers Raigne.

The King had 3 Uncles left him by the Mothers
side, Edward, Thomas and Henry Seymour. Edward was
Lord Protector, and Thomas high Admirall of England;   680
these two Brothers being knit and joyned together in
amity, were like a Bunch of Arrowes not easily broke

asunder, but once dispersed, distracted betwixt
themselves, they made but way for their Adversaries
how to assaile them with little disadvantage.

The two great Dukes of <u>Northumberland</u> and
<u>Suffolke</u>, <u>Dudley</u> and <u>Gray</u>, murmuring that his
Majesties two Uncles should beare such great sway in
the Kingdome (by which their glory seem'd to bee
eclipsed and darkned) sought all meanes how to oppose   690
this great united strength of Fraternall love, but
finding that there was no other way left to cast this
yoake from off their necks (which their Ambition held
to be intolerable) but onely by making a disjunction
of that brotherly love which had so long continued,
and doubting how to worke it by their Servants, tooke
a neerer course to effect it by their wives, and so
to draw their ruines out of their owne bosomes; and
most successively to their owne purposes thus it
happened: Sir <u>Thomas</u> <u>Seymour</u> Admirall and the younger   700
Brother, married the <u>Queene</u> <u>Dowager</u> (whose hap it was
of all the rest to surviue her husband). She
contested with her Sister in Law for precedence and
priority of place. Both were privately encouraged,
both swell'd alike with spleene, neither would give
way to other. The one claim'd it as she had beene

once Queene, the other challeng'd it as she was the
present wife of the Protector. The two Dukes were as
fuell to this fire new kindled betwixt the women;
Dudley incenseth the one privately, Gray encourageth   710
the other secretly. The wives set their husbands at
odds by taking their parts; the Gordian knot of
brotherly love is thereupon dissolved.

Northumberland and Suffolke take hold of this
advantagious occasion, insomuch that within a short
time after, the Admirall was questioned for Treason,
by consent of his brother condemned in Parliament,
and his head struck off at the Tower-hill March 20,
1549, his Brother the Protector with his owne hand
signing the warrant for his death. The one being   720
thus removed, there was now lesse difficulty to
supplant the other. In the same month of February in
which his brother lost his head, was the Protector
committed to the Tower by the Lords of the Councell.
Many Articles especially touching the government of
the State were commenced against him, but the yeare
after, upon his submission to the Lords, and
intercession made for him by the King, hee was
released. This proved but a Lightning before death;
his great and potent Adversaries still prosecute   730

their malice against him, insomuch that not long
after, calling him to a second accompt, when he had
acquit himselfe of all such Articles of Treason as
could bee inferred against him, hee was in a tryall
at Guild-hall convicted of Felony, and on the 22 of
January was beheaded on the Tower-Hill.

These two next Kinsmen to the King, the proppes
and stayes on which the safety of his minoritie
leaned, the hinges on which the whole State turned,
being thus cut off, it was a common feare and   740
generall presage through the whole Kingdome that the
two Uncles being dead, the Nephew would not survive
long after, and so accordingly it happened; for now
all such Gentle-men and Officers as the Protector had
preferred for the Kings attendance, were suddenly
removed, and all such as were the Favourites of the
two Dukes, onely suffered to come neere his person.

In the Interim was the Match concluded betwixt
the Lord Guilford Dudley, Son to the Duke of
Northumberland and the Lady Jane Gray daughter to the   750
Duke of Suffolke. Not long after the King fell sicke
and dyed the 6 of July in the 7th yeare of his
Princely government, and on the tenth of the same
month was proclaymed Queene the Lady Jane. It is to

this day a question both how he dyed and where hee
was buryed, yet others say hee lyes buried at
Westminster. He was a Prince of that hope, that it
would seeme improper thus to leave his honour in the
dust uncharacterized.

Hee was studious for the propagation of the   760
Gospell, the refining and establishing of true
Religion, the foundation whereof his Father had
projected. Images hee caused to be demolished and as
Idolatrous, to be taken out of all Churches within
his Dominions; the learned men of his time hee
encouraged and commanded them to open and expound the
Scriptures, caused the Lords Supper to bee
administred in both kinds unto his people. In the
third yeare of his Reigne, by Parliamentall Decree
hee abolished the Masse, commanded the Liturgie to be   770
made, and our Common prayer and Service to be read in
the English tongue. Hee was acute in witt, grave in
censure, mature in Judgement, all which concurring in
such tender yeeres, were beyond admiration. In the
liberall Arts so frequent, that they appeared rather
innate and borne with him, then either acquired by
teaching or study. All the Port-Townes and Havens in
England, Scotland and France hee had ad unguem; not

the least punctilio of any State affaires past beyond

his observation, nor did hee commit such observations   780

to memory, but had a chest every yeare for the

reservation of such Acts as past the councell board,

himself keeping the key. Hee would appoynt certain

hours to sit with the Master of Requests, only to

dispatch the cause of the Poore. Hee was the

Inchoation and Instauration of a glorious Church and

Commonweale. Hee was perfect in the Latine, Greeke,

Italian, French and Spanish tongues, and (as Cardanus

reports) was well seene in Logicke, and the

Principles of naturall Philosophy, no stranger to   790

Musicke singing at first sight; in Melancthon's

common-places hee was conversant, and all Cicero's

workes, with a great part of Titus Livius; two of

Isocrates Orations hee translated out of the

Originall into Latine. Hee was facetious and witty,

as may appeare in the fourth yeare of his reign, and

thirteenth of his age; being at Greenewich on St.

Georges day, comming from the Sermon with all the

Nobility in State correspondent for the day, said, My

Lords, I pray you what Saint is St. George, that wee   800

so much honour him heere this day? The Lord

Treasurer made answere, If it please your Majesty, I

did never in any History read of St. George, but
onely in Legenda aurea, where it is thus set downe,
that St. George out with his sword and ran the Dragon
through with his speare. The King having something
vented himselfe with laughing, replyed, I pray you my
Lord, and what did hee with his sword the while?
That I cannot tell your Majesty, said hee. To
conclude, hee was so well qualified, that hee was not   810
onely the forwardest Prince of all his Auncestors,
but the sole Phoenix of his time. Dic mihi musa
virum, shew me such another. As hee began and
continued hopefully, so hee ended Religiously. Being
fallen sicke of a Plurisie, some say consumption of
the lungs, having made his peace with God and the
world, he lifted up his eyes and hands to heaven,
prayed to himselfe, thinking none to have heard him,
after this manner:

Lord deliver mee out of this miserable life, and   820
take me among thy chosen; howbeit, not my will, but
thy will be done. Lord, I commit my Spirit to thee.
O Lord thou knowest how happie it were for me to be
with thee; yet for thy chosens sake send me life and
health, that I may truly serve thee. Oh my Lord God,
blesse thy people, and save thine inheritance; Oh

Lord God save thy chosen people of England, defend
this Land from Papistry, and maintaine thy true
Religion, that I and thy People may praise thy holy
name, for thy Sonne Jesus Christ's sake. To which 830
hee added: Oh, I faint, have mercy on me O Lord, and
receive my Spirit. With which ejaculation his life
ended, not without suspition of poyson delivered him
in a Nose-gay; but the divilish Treason not being
enquired after, never came to light.

The Lady Mary being at the time of the Kings
death at Hunsdon in Hertfordshire, was much perplexed
with the newes of the Proclamation of the Lady Jane
as Queene of England; but more especially
understanding that it was done by the consent of the 840
whole Nobility. Hereupon the Suffolke men assemble
themselves about her, not liking such shuffling in
State, profer'd their free and voluntary service
towards the attaining of her lawfull inheritance;
this being bruited at Court, the great Duke of
Northumberland having a large Commission granted, and
signed with the great Seale of England, by the vertue
thereof raised an Army with purpose to suppress and
surprize the Lady Mary. The designe was no sooner
advanced and on foote, but the Lords in generall, 850

repenting them of so great an injurie done to the
Kings Sister, and the immediate Inheritrix, sent a
Countermand after him. The Nobility forsooke him,
the Commons abandon'd him; so that being come to
Cambridge, he with his Sons and some few servants
were left alone, where notwithstanding he and his
associates proclaimed the Lady Mary Queene of England
in the Market-place. Yet for all this hee was
arrested of high treason in the Kings Colledge; from
thence brought to the Tower, and on a Scaffold on the   860
Hill the 12 day of August lost his head. This was
the end of the great Duke of Northumberland. Now
those two great opposing Dukes, Somerset and
Northumberland, whose unlimited Ambitions England and
the governement therof could not satiate, one peece
of ground containes them: they lye quietly together
in one small bed of earth before the Altar in St.
Peters Church in the Tower, betwixt two Queenes,
wives of King Henry the 8th, Queene Anne and Queene
Katherine, all foure beheaded. All their greatnesse   870
and magnificence is covered over with these two
narrow words, Hic iacet. Northumberland overthrew
Somerset and raised himselfe upon his Ruines. Mary,
who was friend to neither, but indifferent to both,

easily dispenced with the cutting off <u>Northumberland</u>,
thinking herselfe to stand more firme by his fall and
ruine.

The Lady <u>Elizabeth</u>, residing at her Mannour in
the Country, much lamented the death of her Brother,
being strangely perplexed in her mind as not knowing   880
by any probable conjecture what these strange
passages of State might come to. But considering
that amongst these tempestuous stormes, her Sister
<u>Marie's</u> and her owne were now at an Adventure in one
bottome, she resolutely first ayded her Sister with
500 men, her selfe the formost, <u>prima ibi ante omnes</u>;
then the storme being over, shee attended her
Majestie in her <u>Barge</u> to the <u>Tower</u>, where was
released the Duke of <u>Norfolke</u>, the Lord <u>Courtney</u>, and
Dr. <u>Gardiner</u>. Soone after, divers Bishops suspended   890
in the dayes of her Brother <u>Edward</u> were restored:
viz. Dr. <u>Gardiner</u> to <u>Winchester</u>, and <u>John Poynet</u> put
out; Dr. <u>Bonner</u> to <u>London</u>, and <u>Nicholas Ridley</u>
confin'd; <u>John Day</u> to <u>Chichester</u>, and <u>John Scory</u>
excluded; Dr. <u>Tonstall</u> to <u>Durham</u>; Dr. <u>Heath</u> to
<u>Worcester</u>, <u>John Hooper</u> excluded, and committed to the
<u>Fleete</u>; Dr. <u>Vesey</u> to <u>Exeter</u>, and <u>Miles Coverdale</u>
cashier'd. The miserable face of a wretched Kingdome

began now to appear. They that could dissemble
their Religion, tooke no great care how things went;   900
but such whose consciences were joyned to truth,
perceiving that the Lamps of the Sanctuary began to
shine dim, seeing those bright Tapers pull'd out of
their sockets and extinguished, concluded that coles
were now kindled which would prove the destruction of
many a good Christian, which accordingly happened.

From the Tower of London the Queene rode through
the City towards her Pallace at West-minster. The
Lady Elizabeth, to whom all this while shee shewed a
pleasant and gracious out-side, rode in a Chariot   910
next after her drawne with sixe Horses trapt in
cloath of silver, the Chariot being covered with the
same, wherein sate only to accompany her, the Lady
Anne of Cleve.

The fifth day of October shee was crown'd at
West-minster by Stephen Gardiner, Bishop of
Winchester (Dr. Thomas Cranmer being at that time in
the Tower). The Lady Elizabeth was most Princely
attended at her Sisters Coronation. Five dayes after
began the Parliament, wherein besides the   920
supplantation of the reformed Religion, Guilford
Dudley and the Lady Jane his wife lately proclaymed

Queene, were both arraigned and convicted of treason.
As for the Lady Jane, how unwilling shee was to take
the imperiall dignitie upon her, doth appeare by this
letter following sent to her Father a little before
her death.

Father, although it hath pleased God to hasten my
death by you, by whom my life should rather have been
lengthened, yet can I so patiently take it, that I   930
yeeld God more hearty thanks for shortning my wofull
dayes, than if all the world had beene given into my
possessions with life lengthened at my owne will.
And albeit I am very well assured of your impatient
dolours, redoubled many wayes, both in bewayling your
owne wo, and especially (as I am informed) my wofull
estate; yet my deare father (if I may without offence
rejoyce in my owne mishaps) herein I may account my
selfe blessed, that washing my hands with the
innocence of my fact, my guiltless blood may cry   940
before the Lord, mercie to the innocent. And yet
though I must needes acknowledge that being
constrained, and (as you know well enough)
continually assayed, yet in taking upon me, I seemed
to consent, and therein grievously offended the
Queene and her Lawes; yet do I assuredly trust that

this my offence towards God is so much the lesse, in
that being in so Royall estate as I was, my enforced
honour never mingled with mine innocent heart. And
thus good father, I have opened unto you the state   950
wherein I presently stand, my death at hand.
Although to you perhaps it may seeme wofull, yet to
mee there is nothing that can bee more welcome than
from this vale of misery to aspire to that heavenly
throne of all joy and pleasure, with Christ my
Saviour, in whose stedfast faith (if it may be
lawfull for the daughter so to write to the father)
the Lord that hath hitherto strengthened you, so
continue to keepe you, that at the last wee may meet
in heaven with the Father, Son, and holy Ghost. I am   960

    Your obedient Daughter till death.

        JANE DUDLEY.

    Shee was no way conscious of those illegall
proceedings practised against the Queene by her owne
and her husbands father. Much griefe there was for
the Lady Jane. The Queene her selfe tooke the
sadnesse of her estate into consideration, gave her
leave to walke in the Queenes Garden, not debarring
her of any pleasant prospect belonging to the Tower,
and had not her father, after first offence remitted,   970

ran headlong into a second, it is generally conceived
shee would have pardoned her life; his mis-councelled
rashnes hasten'd the deaths of these 2 Innocents,
Guilford and Jane. The Statists of that time,
especially such as were addicted to the Romish
faction, held it not policie to suffer any that were
addicted to the contrary faction to live, especially
if they could entrap them, being fallen into any
lapse of the law; therfore upon the twelfth of
February 1554, being the first day of the weeke,   980
Guilford Dudley was brought to the Scaffold on the
Tower-Hill, where having with great penitence
reconcil'd himself to God, with a settled and
unmooved constancie patiently subjected himselfe to
the stroke of death. The head with the body still
bleeding, were both laid together in a Cart, and
brought into the Chappell within the Tower, even in
the sight of this sad and sorrowfull Lady, the object
striking more terrour then the sight of that fatall
Axe, by which her selfe was presently to suffer   990
death. Being instantly led to the Greene within the
Tower, and mounted on a Scaffold, with a cheerefull
and undaunted countenance shee spake as followeth.

   Good People, I am come hither to dye, and by a

Law I am condemned to the same. My offence against the Queene was onely in consent to the device of others, which now is deemed treason; yet it was never of my seeking, but by counsell of those who should seeme to have further understanding of things then I, which knew little of the Law, and much lesse of titles to the Crowne, but touching the procurement thereof by mee, or on my behalfe, I doe wash my hands in Innocency thereof, before God and the face of you all this day. And therewithall she mooved her hands, wherein shee had a Booke, and then proceeded thus: I pray you all good Christian People beare me witnesse that I dye a true Christian Woman, and that I looke to be saved by no other meanes then by the mercy of God in the bloud of his onely Sonne Jesus Christ. I confesse that when I did know the word of God, I neglected it, and loved my selfe and the world, and therfore this plague and punishment is justly and worthily happened upon mee for my sinnes; yet I thanke God of his goodnesse that hee hath given me a time and respite to repent, and now good people whilst I am alive, I pray you assist mee with your Prayers.

    As soone as shee had thus spoken, she humbly

1000

1010

kneeled downe and rehearsed the one and fiftieth
Psalme in <u>English</u>, then she raysed her selfe upon her   1020
feete, and delivered her Booke to Mr. <u>Bridges</u>, who
was then <u>Lieftenant</u> of the <u>Tower</u>. Beginning to untie
her gowne to prepare her selfe for death, the
Executioner offered to help her, but she turning her
selfe to the two Gentlewomen that then attended her,
was by them disroabed both of her gowne and other
attires. Then the Heads-man kneeled downe to aske
her forgivenes, to whom she replyed, <u>The Lord forgive</u>
<u>thee, and I doe, and I entreate thee to dispatch mee</u>
<u>as soone as thou canst</u>. Then kneeling againe, she   1030
looked suddenly backe and said, <u>will you take it</u>
<u>before I lie downe</u>? He answered, <u>No, Madame</u>. Then
she tyed her handkercher before her eyes, and being
blindfold, shee felt about for the Blocke, and said
twice, <u>Where is it</u>? Then laying her necke upon it,
shee stretched forth her body, and said, <u>Lord Jesus</u>
<u>into thy hands I commend my spirit</u>. The Axe met with
the last word, and she expired. Never was a Ladies
fall more deplored, and herein it was remarkable:
Judge <u>Morgan</u>, who gave the sentence of her death   1040
presently fell mad, and in all his distracted fitts
cryed out continually, <u>take away the Lady Jane, take</u>

<u>away</u> the <u>Lady</u> <u>Jane</u> <u>from</u> <u>me</u>, and in that extreame
distemperature of passion, ended his life. Some
report that the Lady <u>Jane</u> was young with Child at the
time of her departure, but though her Romish
opposites were many, and the times bloudy, Christian
Charity may perswade us that they would not use such
inhumanity against so great a person. She was indeed
a Royall Lady, indued with more vertues then are   1050
frequently found in her Sexe; in Religion and Piety
praecellent: her devoute Prayer to God, and Oration
to the People, demonstrated no lesse at the time of
her Execution. Shee was but 16 yeares of age, of
inforc'd honors so unambitious that shee never
attired her selfe in Regall Ornaments, but
constrainedly and with teares. Whilst shee was
Prisoner in the <u>Tower</u> these subsequent verses were
found written on the wall with a Pinne.

<u>Non</u> <u>aliena</u> <u>putes</u>, <u>homines</u>   1060

<u>quae</u> <u>obtingere</u> <u>possint</u>:

<u>Sors</u> <u>hodierna</u> <u>mihi</u>,

<u>cras</u> <u>erit</u> <u>illa</u> <u>tibi</u>.

<u>Thinke</u> <u>nothing</u> <u>strange</u>

<u>that</u> <u>doth</u> <u>on</u> <u>man</u> <u>incline</u>:

> This day my lot is drawne,
>
> Tomorrow thine.

And thus:

> Deo iuvante, nil nocet
>
> livor malus.
>
> Et non iuvante, nit iuvat
>
> labor gravis.
>
> Post tenebras spero lucem.
>
> God on our side, vaine is
>
> all strifes intention.
>
> And God oppos'd, bootlesse
>
> is all prevention.
>
> After night, my hope
>
> is light.

1070

There be extant of her workes in the English
tongue, a learned Epistle to Mr. Harding, Chaplaine
to the Duke of Suffolke her Father, formerly a stout
Champion in King Edwards dayes, but now a Renegado
from the Faith.

1080

A Colloquy with one Fecknam a Priest, two nights
before her death, about Faith and the Sacraments.

An Epistle to her Sister written in the end of
the New Testament in Greeke, sent the night before
she dyed.

As for the Duke of <u>Suffolke</u> her Father, I can 1090
parallell his betraying to none so properly as to the
Duke of <u>Buckingham</u> in the Reigne of <u>Richard</u> the
Third. As the one had a <u>Banister</u>, the other had an
<u>Underwood</u>, a man raysed by him onely to a competent
estate, unto whose trust and gard hee committed his
Person, was by him conveyed into a hollow tree,
morning and evening relieved with sustenance by him,
every time of his appearance renewed his confidence
unto him, and engaged himselfe with millions of
oathes for the performance of his truth and fidelity; 1100
yet easily corrupted with some small quantity of
gold, and many large promises, <u>Judas</u>-like betrayed
his Master, discovered him, and delivered him up to
the Earle of <u>Huntington</u>, under whose conduct hee was
with a strong guard conveyed through <u>London</u> to the
<u>Tower</u>, arraigned and convicted of Treason in the
great Hall at <u>Westminster</u>, and upon the 12 of the
month of <u>February</u> wherein the Daughter expired, was
the Father beheaded on the <u>Tower-Hill</u>.

<u>Northumberland</u> and his Sonne <u>Guilford</u>, <u>Suffolke</u> 1110
with his Daughter <u>Jane</u> being thus cut off, <u>paries</u>
<u>nunc proximus ardet</u>, it was generally fear'd that the
Lady <u>Elizabeth's</u> turne would bee next. The Queene

was no sooner Crown'd, but shee sleighted her, and
removed her into the Countrey. The good Lady was in
the meane time much troubled to see how Bethel lay in
the dust unregarded, and Babel onely exalted, true
Religion dejected, and Superstition advanced, but
more especially understanding that her self was the
butt, and her life the mark they aymed at; yet the   1120
snare was broken, the sword was turned into their
owne bosomes, she pass'd the storme, and at last
arrived safely to the joy of all true hearted
Christians.

This Birth of Ours is but an entrance into this
Life, where in the sight of Heaven wee must endure
for a tryall of our valor, the furious shocks of many
fierce encounters. Hee that sojournes in the Camp of
this life, must not hope for Holy-dayes; his travaile
can have no rest, his labour can have no end; no   1130
Countrey but can yeeld a Pharoh to destroy him, no
Clime but can afford a Herod to pursue him. The
allusion needs no further illustration; the Troubles
of the Lady Elizabeth will make a perfect Comment.
Shee swamme to the Crowne through a Sea of Sorrow,
and having obtained it, how dangerously was her life
insidiated by Popish Assassines? There wanted not a

Jesuiticall <u>Mariana</u> to perswade treason, nor a bloudy

<u>Raviliacke</u> to performe it: then the Pope menaced her

with his Bulls abroad; now the Bishop of <u>Winchester</u>,   1140

the Popes Agent, endeavours to supplant her with

Warrants at home; now she lives captivated to an

incensed Sisters indignation, hurryed from one place

to another, from post to piller.

<u>Quocunque aspicio nihil est</u>

<u>nisi pontus et aër.</u>

<u>The Sea of her Sorrow is so broad and spacious, I can</u>

<u>see no shore, discry no land at all.</u>

Shee was greatly stomack't by <u>Stephen Gardiner</u>,

Bishop of <u>Winchester</u>, and other Romists as well of   1150

the Laity as the Clergie, who studyed by all meanes

possible, not onely to supplant her from the Queenes

love, but to deprive her of her life, the first being

the way to the second; for the better effecting

whereof with the more speed and safety, Fortune

seemed thus to smile upon their enterprise. Sir

<u>Thomas Wiat's</u> insurrection and suppression both

hapning within some few weeks, but being over, and

many having suffered for the same, others were

likewise had in suspition by the Clergie, especially   1160

those whom they termed of the new Religion. Here the

traine is laid for the Lady, the net is spread, they
thinke now all sure; but the Phoenix they aym'd at
was delivered from the hands of the fowler.

This which at the first was in the Queene but
meere suspition, by Bishop Gardiners aggravation grew
after into her high indignation; insomuch that a
strict Commission was sent downe to Ashridge, where
shee then sojourned, to have her with all speede
removed from thence, and brought up to London, there   1170
to answere all such criminall Articles as could be
objected against her.

The Charge was committed to Sir John Williams,
Lord of Tame, Sir Edward Hastings, and Sir Thomas
Cornewallis, all three Councellors of State, and for
the better accomplishment of the Service, a guard of
two hundred and fifty horsemen were attendant on
them.

The Princesse was at the same time dangerously
sicke and even almost to death. The day was quite   1180
spent, and the evening come on; newes being brought
unto her by her servants (much affrighted) that so
great a strength had begirt her house, and in such a
time when her innocence could not so much as dreame
of any thing dangerous that might be suggested

against her, it bred in her howsoever no small
amazement. But ere shee could well recollect her
selfe, a great rapping was heard at the Gate; shee
sending to demand the cause thereof, in stead of
returning an answer, the Lords stept into the House   1190
without demanding so much as leave of the Porter, and
comming into the hall where they met Mistris Ashley,
a Gentlewoman that attended her, they will'd her to
informe her Lady that they had a message to deliver
her from the Queene. The Gentlewoman went up and
told her what they had said, who sent them word back
by her againe (it being then an unseasonable time of
the night, she in her bed and dangerously sicke) to
entreate them, if not in courtesie, yet for modesties
sake to defer the delivery of their Message till   1200
morning. But they without further reply, as shee was
returning to the Princesses Chamber, followed her up
the staires and press'd in after her, presenting
themselves at her bed-side, at which sight shee was
suddenly moved, and told them that shee was not well
pleased with their uncivill intrusion. They, by her
low and faint speech perceiving her debilitie and
weakenesse of body, desired her graces pardon (the
Lord of Tame speaking in excuse of all the rest) and

told her they were sory to find such infirmity upon   1210
her, especially since it was the Queenes express
pleasure that the seventh of that present moneth shee
must appeare before her Majestie at her Court neere
Westminster. To whom shee answered, that the Queene
had not a Subject in the whole Kingdome more ready or
willing to tender their service and loyalty to her
Highnesse, then her selfe; yet hoped withall, in
regard of her present disability, they who were
eye-witnesses of her weake estate, might in their
owne charity and goodnesse dispence with their   1220
extremity of hast. But the hast was such and the
extremitie so great, that their Commission was to
bring her either alive or dead. A sore Commission it
is, said shee. Hereupon they consulted with her
Physitians, charging them on their allegiance to
resolve them, whether she might be removed thence
without imminent perill of her life; upon conference
together they returned answer, that she might
undergoe that journey without death, tho not without
great danger, her infirmity being hazardfull, but not 1230
mortall. Their opinions thus delivered, they told
her Grace that she must of necessity prepare her
selfe for the morrow's journey, and withall, that the

Queene, out of her great favor and care, had sent her
owne Litter; at which words she raysed her self upon
her pillow, thanking the Queene for such grace and
favour extended towards her, telling them that she
would contend with death to tender her life before
her Majestie, and with that small strength she had,
be ready for them in the morning, intreating them to   1240
take such slender provision as her house at such time
could afford, and afterwards to repose themselves in
such Lodgings as were provided for them, and so gave
them the good-night. They tooke their leave with
great respect and reverence to her person, and after
they had set a strong watch upon the House, first
went to supper, and after that to bed.

Early the next morning, by the Rising of the
Sunne, she was mounted into her Litter, and set
onwards towards London. The people as they past the   1250
way, wondring at so great a guard, especially set
upon one they so dearely affected, fearing the more,
the lesse they knew, and because they saw her
conducted as a Prisoner, generally commiserated her
case; some smothering their griefes in silence, and
shaking the head, some expressing it in teares,
others in loud acclamations, that the Lord God

Almighty would safeguard and protect her from all her enemies. In this manner she past onward on her way to Redburne, where she was garded that night; her sicknesse and infirmity had beene guard enough, being able to ride but 3 miles the next day, tarrying that night in Sir Ralph Rowlets house at St. Albones. From thence shee passed to South-Mymms, resting her weary body at Mr. Dods house there, and so the next day to Hie-gate, where being very weake in body and much dejected in mind, she stayed that night, and the next day following; thus was shee brought to the Court, and for full fourteene dayes after remained in a private Chamber altogether solitary and comfortlesse, not so much as suffered to see, much lesse to speake with any friend, onely the Lord Chamberlaine, and Sir John Gage who atended at the dore of her Lodging. Shee had no comforter but her innocence, no companion but her Booke; she was armed with Patience to undergoe the heate of the day, to endure all opposition.

----Quo fata trahunt,

retrahuntque sequemur,

Quicquid erit, superanda

omnis fortuna ferendo est.

1260

1270

1280

None can be brought to so wretched a Condition,
but they may have hope of better fortune. She knew
that the clouds being over, the day wold become
cleare, the Sun but once appearing, those thicke
mists would be soone expelled. Thus she remained a
sorrowfull and dejected Prisoner in the hands of
spleenfull and potent adversaries, brought into so
straight an exigent, either to forsake her faith, or
else to fall under the merciles cruelty of such as   1290
sought her innocent life.

Upon the Friday before Palme-Sunday the Bishop of
Winchester with nine more of the Councel convented
her. Being come before them and offering to kneele,
the Earle of Sussex would by no meanes suffer her,
but commanded a Chayre to bee brought in for her to
sit on. Gardiner, Bishop of Winchester, and then
Lord Chancellor, taking upon him to be the mouth of
the rest, began very sharply to reprove her (as if
shee had beene already convicted) for having a hand   1300
in Wiat's Rebellion, to whom she mildly answered with
a modest protestation, that shee never had the least
knowledge of his practice and proceedings. For
proofe whereof, said shee, when Wyat at his death was
by some malicious enemies of mine demanded whether I

was any way knowing, or accessary to his
insurrection, even at the parting of life and body,
having prepared his soule for heaven, when no
dissimulation can be so much as suspected, even then
he pronounced me guiltlesse; besides the like   1310
question being demanded of <u>Nicholas Throckmorton</u> and
<u>James Crofts</u> at their Arraignment, I was likewise
cleared by them, and being acquitted of all others
(my Lords) would you have mee to accuse my selfe?
After this shee was question'd about a stirring in
the West, rais'd by Sir <u>Peter Carew</u>, but answered to
every particular so distinctly, that they could not
take hold of the least circumstance whereby they
might any way strengthen their accusation; which
<u>Gardiner</u> perceiving, told her that it would bee her   1320
safest course to submit her selfe to the Queene, and
to crave pardon of her gracious Majestie. Wherunto
she answered, that submission confest a crime and
pardon belong'd to a delinquent, either of which
being proved by her, she would then and not till then
make use of his Graces councell. <u>Gardiner</u> told her
she should heare more anon, retiring with the rest of
the Lords to know the Queens further pleasure. They
being gone, she left alone, without either servant to

attend her, or friend to cheere her, began to thinke   1330
with her selfe that beauty was but a flower soone
faded, health a blessing soone altered, favour a
Sun-shine often clouded, riches and glory no better
then broken pillars, but innocency and truth unmoved
Columns. In the midst of these conceptions _Gardiner_
and the rest entred the Chamber and told her that it
was her Majesties pleasure shee must instantly bee
conveyed to the _Tower_, that her houshold was
dissolved, and all her servants discharged, except
her Gentleman Usher, three Gentle-women, and two   1340
Groomes, and that for her guard two hundred Northern
white Coates were appointed that night to watch about
her lodging, and early in the morning to see her
safely delivered into the custody of the _Lieftenant_
of the _Tower_. The very name of _Tower_ strucke a deepe
horror into her, insomuch that the cheerfull blood
forsaking her fresh cheeks, left nothing but ashy
palenesse in her visage. Shee spake these words:
Alasse, my Lords, how comes it that I have so
incensed my Sister, and Soveraigne? If it be held to   1350
be either Criminall or Capitall to bee Daughter to
King Henry, Sister to King Edward of Sacred memory,
or to bee the next in blood to the Queene, I may then

perhaps incurre as well the severity of censure, as
the rigour of Sentence; but otherwise, I here
protest, before heaven and you, I never either in act
or thought have as yet trespass'd against her
Majesty, whose pleasure if it be so, that I must be
confined, and my liberty restrain'd, my humble suite
is unto you, to be Petitioners on my behalfe unto her   1360
Majestie, that I may be sent unto some other place
lesse notorious, that being a Prison for Traytors and
Malefactors in the highest degree. The Earle of
Sussex presently replyed that her request was both
just and reasonable, desiring the rest of the Lords
to joine with him on her behalfe; whereuppon the
Bishop of Winchester cut him off, and told him that
it was the Queenes absolute command, and her pleasure
was unalterable. When, after a little pause, well,
sayd she,   1370

Flebile principium melior

fortuna sequatur.

Injury is but the tryall of our patience,
troubles are onely instructions to teach us wisedome;
by the one falshood from faith may be perceived, by
the other true friends from Traytors may be easily
discerned.

<u>Gutta</u> <u>cavat</u> <u>lapidem</u> ---

<u>hard</u> <u>things</u> <u>may</u> <u>bee</u> <u>mollified</u>, <u>crooked</u> <u>things</u>

<u>straightned</u>; <u>a</u> <u>Rocke</u> <u>will</u> <u>in</u> <u>time</u> <u>relent</u>, <u>and</u> <u>Troy</u>,   1380

<u>though</u> <u>it</u> <u>stands</u> <u>out</u> <u>long</u>, <u>it</u> <u>yeelds</u> <u>at</u> <u>last</u>. <u>Whilst</u>

<u>there</u> <u>is</u> <u>a</u> <u>Sun</u> <u>to</u> <u>set</u>, <u>I</u> <u>wil</u> <u>not</u> <u>despaire</u> <u>of</u> <u>a</u> <u>good</u>

<u>issue</u>: Non omnium dierum Sol occidit, <u>shall</u> <u>bee</u> <u>still</u>

<u>my</u> <u>Comforter</u>. And with these words they all left

her.

That night being spent in pious devotion, the

next day following two Lords brought word that she

must instantly to the <u>Tower</u>, and that the Barge was

ready at the staires to convey her thither; for,

saith one of them (whose name I purposely omit), the   1390

tide will tary for no body. Upon which shee humbly

besought them that shee might onely have the freedome

of one tide more, and that they would solicit the

Queen for so small a favour, whereunto he very

churlishly replyed, that it was a thing by no

possible meanes to bee granted. Then shee desired

that she might write unto the Queene, which he would

not admit. But the Earle of <u>Sussex</u>, being the other

that was sent from the Queene, kneeled unto her, kist

her hand, and said that upon his owne apperill shee   1400

should not onely have the liberty to write, but as he

was a true man unto God and his Prince, he would

deliver her Letter to the Queenes owne hands, and

bring an Answer of the same, whatsoever came thereof.

Whilst shee was writing (for a small peece of

paper could not make sufficient report of her

Sorrowes, being so great in quantity, so

extraordinary in quality), the tyde was spent. Then

they whispered together to take advantage of the

next, but that course was held to be inconvenient, in   1410

regard that it fell out just about midnight. The

difficulty alleadged, was lest that being in the

darke, shee might perhaps be rescued. Therefore the

next day being <u>Palme-Sunday</u>, they repaired unto her

Lodging againe, and desired her to prepare her selfe,

for that was the latest houre of her liberty; and she

must to the Barge presently. Whereunto shee

answered, <u>The Lords will be done</u>. <u>Since it is her</u>

<u>Highnesse pleasure, I am therewith very well</u>

<u>contented</u>. Passing through the Garden and the guard   1420

to take water, shee looked backe to every window, and

seeing none whose lookes might seeme to compassionate

her afflictions, said thus: <u>I wonder whither the</u>

<u>Nobility intends to leade me, being a Princesse, and</u>

<u>of the Royall bloud of England</u>. <u>Alasse, why, being</u>

an harmeles innocent woman, am I thus hurryed to
captivity? The Lord of Heaven knowes whither, for I
my selfe doe not. Great hast was made to see her
safe in the Barge, and much care to have her passe by
London unseene, which was the occasion that both she   1430
and they were engaged to remarkable danger. The Tyde
being young, the Barge-men fear'd to shoot the Bridge
but being forced to it against their wils, the sterne
struck against one of the Arches, and wanting water,
grated against the Channell, with great hazard to be
over-whelmed; but God in his mercy preserv'd her to a
fairer fortune. Shee was landed at the Tower-
stayres, the same intended for Traytors. Loath she
was to have gone ashore there, laying open her
innocent and loyall behaviour both towards the Queene   1440
and present State; but being cut short by the
churlish reply of one who was her convoy, shee went
ashore, and stept short into the water, uttering
these words: I speake it before thee, O God, having
no friend but thee in whom to put my confidence:
heere landeth as true a subject, being Prisoner, as
ever landed at these stayres, since Julius Caesar
laid the first foundation of this structure. Well if
it prove so (said one of the Lords) it will be the

better for you. As shee passed along, the warders   1450
then attending bade God blesse your Grace; for which
some were rebuked in words, others by a mulct in the
purse.

She was then delivered to the charge of the
Constable of the Tower, who received her as his
Prisoner, and told her, that hee would shew her to
her Lodgings; but shee being faint, began to
complaine. The good Earle of Sussex, seeing her
colour began to faile, and she ready to sinke under
his armes, call'd for a Chayre; but the Constable   1460
would not suffer it to be brought. Then shee sate
downe upon a faire stone, at which time there fell a
great shower of raine; the Heavens themselves did
seeme to weepe at such inhumane usage. Sussex
offered to cast his Cloake about her, but she by no
means would admit it. Then the Lieftenant, Mr.
Bridges, entreated her to withdraw her selfe from the
violence of the storme into some shelter, to whom she
answer'd, I had better to sit here then in a worser
place, for God knoweth, not I, whither you intend to   1470
lead me. At which words, looking upon her Gentleman-
Usher, and seeing his eyes full of teares, shee told
him he did not well to disconsolate her with his

sorrow, who had so much griefe of her owne that shee
doubted whether shee had strength enough to support
it.

Being lock'd and bolted in her Lodgings with some
of her servants, she was much daunted and perplexed;
but called to her Gentle-woman for her booke,
desiring God not to suffer her to lay her foundation   1480
upon the sands, but upon the Rock, whereby all blasts
of blustering weather might not prevaile against her.
Whereunto shee added, The skill of a Pilot is
unknowne but in a tempest, the valour of a Captaine
is unseene but in a battell, and the worth of a
Christian is unknowne but in tryall and temptation.
This earthly Globe, O Lord, is but a Theater on which
thou hast placed us, to get some proofe from hence of
our sufficiencie. Death will assaile us, the world
will entice us, the flesh will seeke to betray us,   1490
and the Divell ready to devoure us. But all this and
much more shall never deject my spirits; for thou, O
King of Kings, art my Spectator, and thy Son Christ,
my Saviour Jesus, hath already undergone these tryals
for my encouragement. I will therefore come boldly
to the throne of Grace; there it is, I am sure, that
I shall find comfort in this time of neede. Though

an Hoast should encampe against mee, my heart shall
not feare; though warre should rise against mee, in
this will I be confident. Thou Lord art my light and   1500
my salvation, whom shall I feare? Thou Lord art the
strength of my life, of whom shall I be affraid? In
this Interim the Lords tooke advice about a more
strict watch and ward to be set upon her, all
agreeing that it should be exactly performed. But
the good Earle of Sussex was very passionate to heare
all this, and said, My Lords, my Lords, let us take
heede, and doe no more then our Commission will well
beare; consider that she was the King our Masters
Daughter, and therefore let us use such dealing, as   1510
may hereafter prove answerable. The other Lords
agreed to his words, saying, it was well spoke of
him, and so for that time departed.

   Two dayes after, Gardiner, making use of the
Queenes name and authority, caused Masse to bee
inforcedly said and sung before her, which seemed to
be the greatest tryall shee had till that time
endured, but necessity having no law, shee was forced
to give way to it, and not unadvisedly; that spirit
is prodigious, which rather than shake hands with   1520
inconveniencie would cast it self into the jawes of

danger. Shee with a setled countenance swallowed
downe, upon extremity, the bitter potion of
indignity: shee would rather bow then breake; rather
strike sayle, then perish in the storme. The
greatnesse of her mind gave place to the weakenesse
of her meanes; because shee could not harbor where
shee would, she anchored where shee might with best
security.

Philip of Spaine being interressed in this Story   1530
as one whom God used for an instrument to preserve
the Lady Elizabeth (all those that interposed his
comming into the Kingdome being cut off, namely, the
Duke of Suffolke, Sir Thomas Wyat, with all his
confederacie, and the much suspected Lady Elizabeth
being under safe custody in the Tower), I hope it
will not bee impertinent to impart somwhat of his
landing, Marriage and Coronation.

On the twentieth day of July, Anno 1554, hee
arrived at South-hampton, and was there honourably   1540
met and received by the Queenes Counsell, and the
greatest part of the Nobility. At his first setting
foote on Land, the Garter was presented to him, and
fastned about his Legge. Before hee would enter into
any house, hee went first to the Church of Holy-Rood,

there to give thankes for his prosperous and
successfull Voyage. Having spent about halfe an
houre in devotion, he mounted on a goodly Jennet,
richly Caparison'd, sent to him that morning from the
Queen, and rod backe againe to his Lodging, neere   1550
adjoyning to the Watergate.

The Monday following, he left South-hampton, and
being most honourably attended by the Nobility and
Gentry of England, hee rode toward Winchester; but by
reason of much raine that fell that day, the journey
seemed lesse pleasant.

The next day, betwixt sixe and seaven in the
Evening, hee was there received magnificently, and
rode to Church before hee saw his Lodgings. Lowd
Musicke sounded at his alighting; the Bishop of that   1560
Sea, with foure others, met him at the Church-dore,
with Priests, Singingmen, and Choristers, attired in
rich Copes, with three faire Crosses borne before
them. At his first entrance into the Church, hee
kneeled downe to pray; which done, he arose and went
under a Canopye from the West dore up to the Quire.
Perceiving the Sacrament, hee put off his hat to doe
it reverence, then entred into a goodly traverse hung
with rich Arras and there kneeled againe, till the

Chancellour began Te Deum, and all the Quire   1570

seconded. That done, hee was brought thence by

Torch-light, going on foote to his Lodgings, where

the Queens guard attended on him. All the way as he

passed along he turned himselfe to the people on both

sides, with a pleasant countenance.

After Supper certaine of the Councell brought him

to the Queene by a private way. Shee received him

both graciously and lovingly. They had conference

together about halfe an houre in the Spanish tongue,

which ended, he tooke his leave and was conducted   1580

back to his Lodging.

Upon Tuesday following, about three in the

afternoone, he came from his Lodging on foot,

accompanyed by the Lord Steward, the Earles of Derby

and Pembrooke, with other Lords and Gentlemen, as

well strangers as English. Hee was all in blacke

Cloath; he shewed himselfe freely and openly to all

men. At his entrance into the Court, lowd Musique

plaid. The Queene met him in the great Hall, and

kissed him in the presence of all the people, and   1590

taking him by the right hand, they went up together

into the great Chamber of Presence, and talked

together about a quarter of an houre. Hee then tooke

his leave of her Majesty, went to the Cathedrall to heare _Even-song_, from thence was conveyed to his Lodgings with torch-light.

On St. _James_ day, being the Tutelary Saint of _Spaine_, _July_ 25, the King and Queene came from their Lodgings towards the Church, all on foote, richly attired in gownes of Cloth of gold, set with Stones   1600 and Jemms, hee with his Gard and shee with hers, each of them having a sword borne before them, that of hers by the Earle of _Derby_, the other of his by the Earle of _Pembrooke_. Being come into the Church, he went to one Altar and she to another, both hanged with Curtaines of Cloth of gold, which being after drawn it was thought that they were there shriven; then they resumed their places, and being met, courteously saluted each other, hee being at that time bare-headed. Sixe Bishops went to the place   1610 prepared for the Ceremony; the King was on the left hand, and shee on the right. _Winchester_ celebrated the Nuptials first in _Latine_, then in _English_; the marriage Ring was a plaine hoop Ring of gold without any Stone. The Ceremonies being consummate, they both went hand in hand together; comming to the Altar, they both kneeld a while with each of them a

lighted Taper in their hand. After the Masse was
ended, the King of <u>Heralds</u> openly in the Church
proclaimed their Majesties King and Queene, with   1620
their Stiles and Titles, as followeth.

<u>Philip</u> and <u>Mary</u>, by the Grace of God, King and
Queene of <u>England</u>, <u>France</u>, <u>Naples</u>, <u>Jerusalem</u>, and
<u>Ireland</u>, Defendors of the Faith, King and Queene of
<u>Spayne</u>, <u>Sicilia</u>, <u>Leon</u>, and <u>Arragon</u>, Arch-Dukes of
<u>Austria</u>, Dukes of <u>Millaine</u>, <u>Burgundie</u>, and <u>Brabant</u>,
Countees of <u>Hasborough</u>, <u>Flanders</u> and <u>Tirroll</u>, Lords
of the <u>Ilands</u> of <u>Sardinia</u>, <u>Majorca</u>, <u>Minorca</u>, of the
<u>Firme-land</u>, and the great <u>Ocean Sea</u>, Palatines of
<u>Henault</u>, and the holy <u>Empire</u>, Lords of <u>Freezeland</u> and   1630
<u>Ireland</u>, Governours of all <u>Asia</u> and <u>Affrica</u>.

The Trumpets ceasing, the King and Queene came
forth, hand in hand royally attended, and dyned
together openly in the Hall at one Table.

On the eighteenth of <u>August</u> they came to <u>Suffolke</u>
place in <u>Southwarke</u>; there they dined, after dinner
roade over the Bridge, and so through <u>London</u> to
<u>West-minster</u>. Great Triumphes met them by the way,
with the presentation of divers Pageants and Shewes,
having reference to their Persons, and the great joy   1640
conceived of their Royall Marriage.

Heere is one Sister in her Majesty, the other in
misery; the one upon her Throne, the other in the
Tower, every day expecting some newes or other of her
death. It would make a pittifull and strange Story,
to relate what examinations and rackings of poore men
there was to finde but out that knife which might cut
her throat. Gardiner, with divers others of the
Councell came to have a second examination of her,
demanding what conference shee had with Sir James   1650
Crofts, being then a Prisoner in the Tower, and
brought into her presence on set purpose to confront
her, alleadging that the speech which they had
privately was about her removall from Ashridge to
Dunnington Castle. At the first shee was somewhat
amazed, not remembring that shee had any such House;
but having recollected her selfe, I doe remember, my
honourable Lords, that I have such a House; but me
thinkes you doe me great injury, thus to presse,
examine, and produce every petty meane Prisoner   1660
against mee. If they have beene Delinquents and done
ill, let them at their owne perill answer it, but
neither number mee nor joyne mee with such
malefactors and offendors. As touching my Remove to
Dunnington, my officers, and you Sir James Crofts

being then present, can wel testifie whether any rash
or unbeseeming word did at that time passe my lippes,
which might not have well become a faithfull and
loyall Subject. But what is all this to the purpose,
my Lords? Might I not without offence goe to my   1670
House at all times when I best pleased? At which
words the Earle of Arundell kneeling downe, said,
Your Grace saith truth, and for mine owne part I am
much greeved that you should bee thus troubled about
matters of no greater moment. Well my good Lords
(said she) you sift me very narrowly, but you can doe
no more unto me then God in his divine providence
hath appointed, and to him onely will I direct my
prayers to forgive you all. Sir James Crofts kneeled
unto her, being heartily sory that ever hee should   1680
see that day to bee a witnesse against her, taking
God to witnesse that hee never knew any thing by her
worthy of the least suspition; yet notwithstanding
there appeared not the least probability of any
fault, nothing but meere suspitions and suggestions
could bee objected, shee was still kept close
Prisoner. The Constable of the Tower then Lord
Chamberlaine, would not suffer her owne servants to
carry up her dyet, but put it into the hands of rude

and unmannerly Soldiers, of which shee complaining   1690
to her Gentleman-Usher to have that abuse better
ordered, the Lieftenant not onely denyed to see it
remedied, but threatned him with imprisonment if hee
againe did but urge such a motion. Neither would hee
suffer her own Cooks to dress her dyet, but mingled
his owne servants with hers. Violent he was in the
persecution of her innocence; his malice was sharpe
and keene against her, insomuch that shee was ready
to sinke under the heavy and insupportable burthen of
his cruelty, but that God who still protected her,   1700
raised up an instrument to take off the edge of his
so violent oppression. The Lord Shandoys, then one
of her Keepers, moved the Lords of the Councell on
her behalfe, and by his only intercession shee had
the freedome of the Queens Lodgings, and liberty to
open her Casement to take in the Ayre, which before
that time could by no meanes be possibly granted.

In the interim a Warant came downe under Seale
for her execution. Gardiner was the onely Daedalus
and inventor of the engine, but Mr. Bridges had the   1710
honour of her delivery; for hee no sooner received
the Warrant, but mistrusting false play, presently
made hast to the Queen. Shee was no sooner informed,

but renounced the least knowledge thereof, called
Gardiner and others, whom shee suspected, before her,
blamed them for their inhumane usage of her, and
tooke advice for her better security; and thus was
Achitophels bloudy device prevented.

Soone after, on the fift of May, the Constable of
the Tower was discharged, and one Sir Henry   1720
Benningfield succeeded in his place, a man altogether
unknowne to her Grace, and therefore the more to be
feared. The sodainnes of the change did at that time
somewhat daunt her; but the same power which remooved
the one out of his Lieftenantship, at the very same
time released her out of her close and strict
imprisonment in the Tower, and from thence conveyed
her to Woodstock, under the conduct and charge of Sir
Henry Benningfield, with whom was joyned in
Commission Sir John Williams, the Lord of Tame, and a   1730
hundred Northren Blew-Coates to attend them. These
presenting themselves before her, shee instantly
apprehended them to bee her new guardians; but at the
sight of Sir Henry, whom shee had never till that
time seene, she sodainly started backe, and called to
one of the Lords, privately demanding of him, whether
the Scaffold were yet standing whereon the innocent

Lady _Jane_ had not long before suffered? Hee resolved
her, that upon his honour it was quite taken downe,
and that no memoriall thereof was now remaining; then   1740
shee beckoned another Noble-man unto her, and asked
of him what Sir _Henry_ was? if hee knew him? or if a
private murther were committed to his charge, whether
hee had not the conscience to performe it? Answer
was made that hee was a man whom the Queene
respected, and the _Chancellour_ much favoured, and
that she should without doubt finde him a man better
qualified then she supposed, both of a stricter
Conscience, and more Christian-like condition. _It is_
well (said shee) _if it prove so._ Shee seemed herein   1750
somthing satisfied, and the rather, because from the
mild aspect of the Lord of _Tame_, shee expected some
comfort; shee perceived compassion in his eye, to
defend her from the countenance of the other, which
prefigured unto her nothing but oppression.

The nineteenth of _May_ shee removed from the
Tower towards _Wood-stocke_, being that night appointed
to lie at _Richmond_, whither they were no sooner come,
and she entred into her Lodgings, but the Souldiers
were placed about her, and all her servants billited   1760
in by- and out-houses; which shee perceiving call'd

her Gentleman Usher fearfully unto her, bad him and
all the rest of her's to pray for her, for shee
doubted that night to be there murdered, and that she
had no hope to survive that morning. Wherewith he
being struck to the heart, said, God forbid that any
such wickednesse should bee intended against your
grace. If it were so, that God who hath thus
favourably supported you hitherto, will defend you
still; he is God omnipotent, God all-sufficient, God   1770
that hath releeved, God that can helpe, God that
never will forsake all such as put their trust in
him. Bee of good courage, let not your Grace be
dejected; though sorrow be heere in the evening, yet
joy will be in the morning. Shee thanked him for his
comfortable advice, and added: Bee mercifull unto me,
O God, be mercifull unto mee, for my soule trusteth
in thee, yea in the shadow of thy wings will I make
my refuge, untill these calamities be overpast.
Hereupon hee departed with teares in his eyes,   1780
leaving her to God, and her selfe; but could not
rest, till hee had acquainted the Lord of Tame with
all such feares as her Grace had conceived. Comming
downe into the Hall, hee found Sir Henry Benningfield
and the Lord of Tame walking together, and having

singled out the Lord of Tame, told him that the cause
of his comming was to bee resolved, whether there
were any secret plot intended against her Grace that
night or no, and if there were, that hee and his
fellowes might know it, for they should account
themselves happy to lose their lives in her rescue.
The Lord of Tame nobly replyed, that all such feares
were needlesse, for if any such thing were attempted,
hee and all his followers would spend their blouds in
her defence. So praise be to God they passed that
night in safety, though with no little griefe of
heart.

The next morning the Countrey people,
understanding which way she was to take her journey,
had assembled themselves in divers places, some
praying for her preservation and liberty, others
presented her with Nose-gayes and such expression of
their loves as the countrey afforded. The
inhabitants of neighbour Villages commanded the Bels
to be rung, so that what with the lowd acclamations
of People, and the sound of Bels, the very Ayre did
Eccho with the preservation of Elizabeth, which being
perceived by Sir Henry Benning-field, hee call'd them
Rebells and Traytors, beating them backe with his

1790

1800

Truncheon; as for the Ringers he made their pates   1810

ring noone before they were releast out of the

stocks. The Princesse intreated him in their

behalfe, and desired that hee would desist from the

rigour used to the people. I cannot by any meanes

suffer (saith he) their clamorous out-cryes, they

grate my eares with their bablings. Besides it is

not tollerable, by vertue of my Commission; and at

every word he spoke hee still had up his Commission,

which the Princess taking notice of, told him that he

was no better then her Gaoler. The very name of   1820

Gaoler moved his patience; but knowing not how to

mend himselfe, he humbly intreated her Grace not to

use that name, it being a name of dishonour, a

scandall to his Gentry. It is no matter (said she)

Sir Henry, me thinkes that name and your nature agree

well together. Let mee not heare of that word

Commission; as oft as you but nominate your

Commission, so oft will I call you Gaoler.

    As shee passed along towards Windsor, divers of

her servants, seeing her passe so sadly by the way,   1830

being such as had beene formerly discharged at the

dissolution of her Houshold, requested her Grace,

that shee would vouchsafe to resolve them whither she

was carryed. To whom shee sent backe an answer in
these two narrow words, Tanquam Ovis.

   She lodged that night at the Deane of Windsors
house, and passed the next day to Mr. Dormers house;
by the way, there was great concourse of People to
see her Grace. The next night shee came to the Lord
of Tame his house, where shee was most nobly   1840
entertained by all the Gentry of the Countrey,
comming to congratulate her safety, to condole her
misery, whereat Sir Henry Benningfield was highly
displeased, and told them that they could not tell
what they did, and were not able to answer the least
part of their actions, informing them that she was
the Queens Prisoner, and no otherwise, advising them
withall, to take heede what they did, and beware of
after-clappes. Whereunto the Lord of Tame made
answer, that hee was well advised of his doings,   1850
being joyned in Commission as well as he, and that he
would warrant both her Graces mirth and entertainment
in his house. Sir Henry being thus opposed, went up
into a Chamber, where was prepared a Chayre, two
Cushions, and a rich Carpet for her Grace to sit in;
but he impatient to see such Princely furniture for
her entertainment, rather then hee should not be

taken notice of, like <u>Erostratus</u> that set the Temple of <u>Diana</u> on fire onely to get him a name, hee presumptuously sate in the Chayre, and called one Barwicke his man to pull off his Bootes; which being knowne over the house, he was well derided for his uncivill behaviour. That night she passed as a welcome guest to the Lord of <u>Tame</u>; but Sir <u>Henry</u> being formerly galled, what with the Royall entertainment of her Grace, and partly by the jeering speeches lately put upon him, hee would not suffer her to sleepe under the sole custody of the Lord of <u>Tame</u>, being in mistrust of his owne shadow, and therefore set a strong watch upon the house.

The next day they came to <u>Woodstock</u>, where shee was no sooner entred, but locked and bolted up as formerly in the <u>Tower</u>. Here her feares grew greater, and her liberty lesse, her Lodgings the meanest and coursest about the house, night and day guarded with rude and uncivill Soldiers. Besides, the Keeper of the house was reputed a notorious Ruffian, of an evill conditioned life, one that waited his opportunity to deprive her of hers, and being encouraged by some great ones then at Court, made divers attempts, but by the immediate hand of God was

1860

1870

1880

still prevented; and for Sir <u>Henry</u> <u>Benning-field</u>, he
was stil the same, omitting not the least occasion to
set his Commission on the Tenterhooks of severity.
In this onely shee espyed some small glimpse of
comfort, that by the means of a worthy Knight of
<u>Oxford-shire</u>, joyned in Commission with Sir <u>Henry</u>,
she had at last the liberty of the Gardens to walke
in, but Sir <u>Henry</u> locked and unlocked the dores
himselfe, not daring to trust any with the keyes.   1890
Whereupon shee said unto him: Why, <u>are</u> <u>not</u> <u>you</u> <u>now</u> <u>my</u>
<u>Gaoler</u>? <u>I</u> <u>beseech</u> <u>your</u> <u>Grace</u> (said hee) <u>doe</u> <u>but</u>
<u>forbeare</u> <u>that</u> <u>word</u>: <u>I</u> <u>am</u> <u>not</u> <u>your</u> <u>Gaoler</u>, <u>but</u> <u>an</u>
<u>Officer</u> <u>appointed</u> <u>by</u> <u>her</u> <u>Majesty</u> <u>to</u> <u>keepe</u> <u>you</u> <u>safe</u>.
<u>God</u> <u>blesse</u> <u>her</u> <u>Majestie</u> (said shee) <u>and</u> <u>from</u> <u>such</u>
<u>officers</u> <u>good</u> <u>Lord</u> <u>deliver</u> <u>mee</u>. Being in the Garden,
she was alwayes employed in Devotion, taken up with
one meditation or other. Not the least pile of
grasse shee trod on but afforded instruction: <u>humus</u>
<u>aut</u> <u>humi</u> <u>repens</u>, grasse or grashopper shee   1900
acknowledged her selfe. Then casting her eyes upon
those goodly Parkes, furnished with tall and stately
Oakes, whose erected tops and large-spreading
branches over-looked the under-woods and lesser
Plants, not so much as admitting any Sun-beame to

reflect upon their Boughes, but such faint
cheque r-spotted light as shined through the
sufferance of their leaves, nor allowing the Raine of
Heaven to fall upon them, onely such as from
superfluity and aboundance drop't from their   1910
branches; to these streight and extending trees, shee
compared the Nobilitie; to the Arbusculae or smaller
Plants, the Commons; but to the Tamarix, the bryer
and bush, the poorest and meanest of the People.
Then conferring the estate of the Honourable with the
condition of the humble, the tempests that shake the
mighty and blow over the meane, as being scituate in
the lesse eminent place, that it is the longest Roab
which contracts the greatest soyle; they that walke
on the tops of Pinnacles are onely in the danger,   1920
whilst those which are upon the ground march more
securely.

Many were the Troubles of this good Lady, her
dangers more. Shee had very neere been burned in her
bed one night had there not beene prevention; she was
in medio ignis, in the midst of a fire kindled, as it
is reported, on set purpose to have consumed her; but
being espyed by a worthy Knight in Oxford-shire to
flame through the boords of her Chamber, was

presently extinguished. Shee was <u>in</u> <u>medio</u> <u>ignis</u>, in   1930

the midst of that fiery tryall. The whole Kingdome

was then enflamed with <u>Bone-fires</u> of Gods Saints.

There was Fire in the Center, Fire all about the

Circumference, Fire at home, Fire abroad, Fire in her

private Chamber, Fire all over the whole Kingdome.

What a dangerous exigent must shee needs come to,

whose life was thus assaulted?

<u>Tu</u> <u>quibus</u> <u>ista</u> <u>legas</u>,

<u>incertum</u> <u>est</u> <u>lector</u>, <u>ocellis</u>,

<u>Ipse</u> <u>equidem</u> <u>siccis</u>   1940

<u>scribere</u> <u>non</u> <u>potui</u>.

Reader, <u>with</u> <u>what</u> <u>eye</u>

<u>canst</u> <u>thou</u> <u>this</u> <u>peruse</u>,

Since <u>writing</u> <u>them</u>, <u>I</u> <u>wept</u>,

<u>and</u> <u>could</u> <u>not</u> <u>chuse</u>.

God, whose breath is as a flaming fire, blasted

all her fiery Adversaries, suspended the violent rage

of al this Fire, and snatched her as a brand out of

the midst thereof, not so much as a haire of her head

being sindged. Being thus delivered out of the hands   1950

of her enemies, she persevered in the service of God

all the dayes of her life; and for the present having

well weighed the danger lately escaped, shee said,

Quid tibi retribuam Domine? What shall I render unto
the Lord for all these blessings so favourably from
time to time bestowed upon me? Then retyring into
her private Chamber, shee thus began to pray:

O Gracious Lord God, I humbly prostrate my selfe
upon the bended knees of my Heart before thee,
intreating thee (for thy Sonnes sake) to be now and   1960
ever mercifull unto me. I am thy worke, the work of
thine own hands, even of those hands which were
nayled to the Crosse for my sinnes; looke upon the
wounds of thy hands, and despise not the worke of thy
hands; thou hast written me downe in thy Booke of
preservation, with thine owne hand. Oh read thine
owne hand writing, and save mee, spare me that speake
unto thee; pardon mee that pray unto thee. The
Griefes I endure, enforce me to speake, the
calamities I suffer impell mee to complaine. If my   1970
hopes were in this Life only, then were I of all
people most miserable; it must needes be so, that
there is another Life, for here they live many times
the longest lives who are not worthie to live at all:
Heere the Israelites make the Brickes, and the
AEgyptians dwell in the houses; David is in want, and
Nabal abounds; Syon is Babilons, Captive. Hast thou

nothing in store for Joseph, but the Stocks? for
Esay, but a Saw? Will not Elias adorne the Chariot
better then the Juniper-tree? Will not John Baptists   1980
head become a Crowne as well as a Platter? Surely
there is great Retribution for the just, there is
fruit for the Righteous; thou hast Palms for their
hands Coronets for their heads, white Robes for their
Bodies; thou wilt wipe all teares from their eyes,
and shew them thy goodnesse in the land of the
living. Oh good and desirable is the shadow of thy
wings (Lord Jesus). There is the safe Sanctuary to
flee unto, the comfortable refreshing of all sinne
and sorrow. Whatsoever Cup of affliction this Life   1990
propines unto me, is nothing to those bitter draughts
thou hast already drunke unto me. Helpe me, O thou
my strength, by which I shall bee raised; come thou
my light, by which I shall be illuminated; appeare
thou glory, to which I shall bee exalted; hasten thou
life through which I shall bee hereafter glorified.
Amen, Amen.

     Thus did shee both devoutly and religiously make
use of all afflictions imposed upon her. Shee ever
laid her Foundation upon that Primum quaerite, which   2000
is the chiefe Corner-Stone both of Divinitie and

Philosophy. But being over-whelmed with an
inundation of Sorrow and Feare, she humbly petition'd
the Councell that they would admit her to write to
the Queene, which at first was prohibited, but
afterwards most lovingly permitted. Sir Henry
Benningfield brought her Pen, Paper and Inke, and
would not so much as depart the Roome whilst shee had
Pen to Paper; and ever when shee was weary of
writing, hee carried her Letters away and brought   2010
them again at his pleasure. But having finished her
Letters, hee said that hee would carry them to Court.
No (said shee) one of my owne shall carry them; I
will trust neither your selfe, nor any that belongs
to you therein. Wherunto he replyed, You are a
Prisoner to the Queene; I hope there is none of your
Servants dares be so bold as to deliver any Letters
of yours to her Majestie, you being in that case.
Yes (quoth shee) I have none that are so dishonest,
but will be as willing to doe for me in that behalfe,   2020
as ever they were. That's true (said he) but my
Commission is to the contrary; I can by no means
suffer it. Her Grace replying againe, said, You
charge mee very often with your Commission, I pray
God you may hereafter answer the cruell dealing used

towards <u>mee</u>. Then hee kneeling downe desired her
Grace to consider, that hee was but a Servant put
only in trust by her Majesty to keepe her safe,
protesting that if the Case were hers, hee would as
willingly observe her Grace, as now hee did the
Queenes Highnesse. For his answer shee returned him
thankes, beseeching God that shee might never stand
in need of such servants as he was; giving him
further to understand that his actions towards her
were neither good nor answerable; nay such, as the
best friends he had could never maintaine. <u>I doubt</u>
<u>not</u> (said hee) <u>but to make good account of my</u>
<u>Actions</u>; <u>there is no remedy but that I must answer</u>
<u>them, and so I wil wel enough, I'le warrant you.</u>
Being angred and vexed with her Graces speeches, hee
kept the Letters foure dayes after they were dated;
but in conclusion, hee was faine to send for her
Gentleman-Usher from the Towne of <u>Woodstocke</u>, and
asked him whether hee durst deliver his Mistris
Letters to the Queene. <u>Yes</u> (said hee) <u>that I dare</u>
<u>and will withall my heart.</u> Then Sir <u>Henry</u> halfe
against his stomacke delivered them unto him.

Not long after, her Grace fell sicke, which the
Queene no sooner heard of, but shee sent Dr. <u>Owen</u> and

2030

2040

Dr. <u>Wendye</u> to visite her. Being come to <u>Woodstocke</u>,   2050

they carefully administred unto her, let her bloud,

and in sixe dayes set her on foote againe, and so

taking their leave of her Grace, return'd to Court

and made a large report both to the Queene and

<u>Councell</u> of her humble behaviour and allegiance

towards them. The Queene no sooner heard it, but

rejoyced at it; her adversaries looked black in the

mouth, not knowing how to mend themselves, but onely

by inciting the Queene against her, telling her that

they much wondred that shee did not submit her selfe,   2060

having offended her Highnesse.

In the <u>Interim</u>, her Grace was much solicited by

divers pretended friends, to submit her selfe to the

Queene, informing her that it would be well taken,

and bee very conducible to her benefit and further

inlargement. The words were no sooner uttered, but

shee most resolutely made answer in this manner: <u>I</u>

<u>will</u> <u>never</u> <u>submit</u> <u>to</u> <u>any</u> <u>one</u> <u>whom</u> <u>I</u> <u>never</u> <u>offended</u> <u>in</u>

<u>all</u> <u>my</u> <u>life</u>. <u>If</u> <u>I</u> <u>am</u> <u>a</u> <u>delinquent</u>, <u>and</u> <u>have</u>

<u>offended</u>, <u>Currat</u> <u>Lex</u>, <u>let</u> <u>the</u> <u>Law</u> <u>take</u> <u>course</u>, <u>I</u>   2070

<u>crave</u> <u>no</u> <u>mercy</u> <u>at</u> <u>all</u>; <u>the</u> <u>law</u> <u>is</u> <u>just</u> <u>and</u> <u>will</u> <u>not</u>

<u>condemne</u> <u>me</u>. <u>My</u> <u>Keeper</u> <u>that</u> <u>locketh</u> <u>mee</u> <u>up</u> <u>day</u> <u>and</u>

<u>night</u>, <u>doth</u> <u>continually</u> <u>molest</u> <u>mee</u>; <u>if</u> <u>I</u> <u>were</u> <u>but</u> <u>as</u>

free from the one, as I am from the other, I should
thinke my selfe most happy; howsoever God in his good
time, will either mollifie his heart, or move some
other to procure my further inlargement.

The Counsell board, especially the adverse party,
were no sooner possess'd with the constancie of her
resolution, but they sent up for Sir Henry Benning- 2080
field her Keeper; no way was unattempted, which might
make for their ends. Great Consultation was held
about a Marriage for her. The Spaniards thought it
most convenient to bee with some Stranger, that she
might have her Portion and so depart the Land; some
thought that not to bee the safest course to send her
abroad. But one Lord and Gardiner resolved upon a
more speedy one: the one said that the King would
never have any quiet Common-wealth in England till
her head were struck off from her shoulders; the 2090
other, My Lords, we have but all this while beene
stripping off the leaves, and now and then lopped a
branch; but till such time as wee strike at the Roote
of Heresie (meaning the Lady Elizabeth) nothing to
purpose can bee effected. God forbid, replyed the
Spaniards, that our King and Master should once
conceive a thought to consent unto such a mischiefe.

And from that day forward they did not let slip the
least opportunity to solicite the King on her
behalfe, informing him that the like honour he could   2100
never obtaine, as he should have by delivering her
out of Prison, which was not long after effected.
Sir Henry Benning-field staying long at Court, made
her jealous that his businesse was not greatly for
her good. During his residence there one Basset, a
Gentleman and great Favourite to the Bishop of
Winchester, came to Blanden-bridge, a mile distant
from Wood-stocke, where met him twenty men well
appointed and secretly arm'd in privy Coates. From
thence they came to the house, ernestly desiring to   2110
speak with the Princesse about serious and important
affaires; but by Gods great providence, Sir Henry her
Keeper had left so strict a charge behind him, that
no living Soule might have access unto her upon what
occasion soever, till his returne, no not though a
messenger were dispatched from the Councell, or the
Queene her selfe, hee should not bee admitted: by
which extraordinary Providence of God, drawing the
meanes of her safety even from the malice of her
adversaries, their bloody enterprize was utterly   2120
disappointed. These things with other of the like

nature being delivered unto her, her doubts and
feares dayly more and more increasing, it is
constantly reported that hearing the Milke-maids
morning and evening singing so sweetly, considering
their hearts to be so light and hers so heavy; their
freedome, her bondage; their delights abroad, her
dangers within, shee wished even from her soule, both
for safety of her person, and security of her
Conscience, that no Royall bloud at all ran in her   2130
veynes, but that she had beene descended from some
meane and humble Parentage.

Queene <u>Mary</u> was bruited to bee with Child, great
thanksgiving was made, and prayers for that purpose
were appointed to bee read in Churches. King <u>Philip</u>
was chosen by a decree in Parliament, Protector of
the Infant, Male or Female, yet notwithstanding hee
greatly favoured the Lady <u>Elizabeth</u>; her adversity
made him very jealous of the English Nation,
apprehending that if they aymed at the life of a   2140
Naturalist, being their Queene and Soveraigns Sister,
they would then make it a small scruple of Conscience
to assault him and his Followers, being meere Aliens
and strangers. Hee did therefore hasten her
enlargement, which happly was granted within few

dayes after; but before her departure from
Wood-stocke, having private notice that one Mr.
Edmond Tremaine and Mr. Smithweeke were on the Racke,
and strictly urged to have accused her innocence, at
her remove from thence shee wrote these two Verses   2150
with her Diamond in a glasse window.

Much suspected by me,

Nothing proved can be.

Quoth Elizabeth

Prisoner.

Immediately after, order came down to bring her
up to Court, whereupon all things were prepared for
the journey. Sir Henry Benningfield with his
souldiers, the Lord of Tame and Sir Henry
Chamberlaine were her guardians on the way. As shee   2160
came to Ricot the wind was so high, that her servants
had much adoe to keepe her cloaths about her; her
hood was blowne from her head twice or thrice,
whereupon shee desired to retyre her selfe to a
Gentlemans house neere adjoyning, to dresse up her
head, which by the violence of the winde was all
unready. The request was reasonable and modest, but
Sir Henry would not by any meanes permit it, insomuch
as shee was faine to alight under a hedge, and there

to trim her selfe as well as shee could. That night   2170
shee lay at <u>Ricot</u>, the next day they journeyed to Mr.
<u>Dormers</u>, and the third to <u>Colebrooke</u>, lying at the
signe of the <u>George</u>. Divers of her Gentlemen came
thither to see her, but by the Queens command were
immediately sent out of the towne, to both their and
her Graces no small heavinesse, being not so much as
suffered to speake to each other. The next day
following her Grace entred <u>Hampton Court</u> on the
Backside, the doores being shut upon her, the
Souldiers in their ancient posture of watch and ward.   2180
She lay there fourteene dayes before any man had
admittance unto her: many were her fears, her cares
doubled. But at length a Sonne of Consolation
appeared: the Lord <u>William</u> <u>Howard</u> came unto her, used
her very honourably, condol'd with her, and rais'd
her dejected Spirits with comfortable speeches,
wherein shee conceived much joy, and requested his
Favourable encouragement, that she might speake with
some of the <u>Councell</u>, which he most lovingly
effected, for not long after came her fast friend the   2190
Bishop of <u>Winchester</u> accompanied with the Lords of
<u>Arondell</u> and <u>Shrewsbury</u>, and <u>Secretary</u> <u>Peter</u>, who
with great humility humbled themselves to her grace.

She was not behind in courtesie, but lovingly
re-saluted them againe, and said: My honourable
Lords, I am glad with all my heart to see your faces,
for mee thinks I have beene kept a great while from
you, desolately alone, committed to the hands of a
strict keeper. My humble Request is to all your
Lordships, that you would bee the happy instruments   2200
of my further inlargment. It is not unknowne unto
you what I have suffered now a long time; I beseech
you therefore to take me into your loving
Consideration. The Bishop of Winchester kneeling
down replied thus: Let mee request your grace but to
submit your selfe to the Queene, and then I doubt not
but that you shall presently enjoy an happy issue of
your desires. No (said she) rather then I will so
doe, I will lye in prison all the dayes of my life;
if ever I have offended her majesty in thought, word,   2210
or deed, then not mercy, but the law is that which I
desire. If I yeeld, I should then speake against my
selfe, confes a fault which was never on my part
intended, by occasion wherof the King and Queene may
then justly conceive an evill opinion of me; no, no,
my Lords, it were much better for me to lye in prison
for the truth, then to be at liberty suspected by my

Prince. She had no sooner uttered the words, but
they al departed, promising to declare her mind to
the Queene.   2220

On the next day the Bishop of Winchester came
unto her againe, and kneeling on his knees, declared,
that the Queene wondred that she should so stoutly
stand out, not confessing to have offended, so that
it should seeme, the Queenes Majesty had wrongfully
imprison'd her. No (said she) I ne're had any such
thought; it may please her Majesty to punish me, as
she thinketh good. Well (quoth he) her Majesty
willed me to tell you, that you must tell another
tale before you are set at Liberty. Alas, (said she)   2230
I had rather bee here in custody with honesty and
truth, then abroade at Liberty suspected by my
Prince, and this that I have said, I will stand to;
for I will never belye my selfe. Why then (said he)
your grace hath the advantage of mee and the rest of
the Lords, for your long and wrong imprisonment.
What advantage I have (said she) God and your own
conscience can best tell, and here before him I
speake it; for that dealing which I have had amongst
you, I seek no remedy, but pray that God may forgive   2240
you all. Amen, Amen, (said he) and so departed.

Seven dayes and nights she continued lockt up in her
lodgings, not so much as having seene the Queene,
though both under one Roofe; yet at last after many
Letters written, long Suite, and great friends made,
she was admitted to the presence of the Queene, whose
face in two yeeres and more she had not seene. King
Philip having before mediated for her, and placed
himselfe unknowne to the Queene behind the hangings
of Arras on purpose to heare the discourse, her grace   2250
about ten of the clock at night was sent for into the
presence; the suddennesse of the message did somwhat
daunt her, especially being at that time of the
night. Whereupon she entreated those that were about
her, to pray for her, and then with the constancy of
her former resolution, shee went towards the
presence, where being entred, finding her Majesty
sitting in her Chaire of State, after three conges,
she humbly fel down upon her knees, praying for the
health, long life and preservation of her Majestie,   2260
protesting her truth, and loyalty towards her person,
notwithstanding whatsoever had been maliciously
suggested to the contrary. Whereunto the Queene very
sharpely answered, Then you will not confesse your
selfe to be a delinquent I see, but stand

peremptorily upon your truth and innocence; I pray
God they may so fall out. If not (replied the
Princesse) I neither require favour nor pardon at
your Majesties hands. Well (said the Queene) then
you stand so stiffly upon your faith and loyalty,   2270
that you suppose your selfe to have been wrongfully
punished and imprisoned. I cannot(said she) nor
must not say so to you. Why then belike (said the
Queene) you will report it to others. Not so
(replied the good Lady) I have borne and must beare
the burthen my selfe, and if I may but enjoy your
Majesties good opinion of me, I shall be the better
enabled to beare it still, and I pray God that when I
shall cease to be one of your Majesties truest and
loyall subjects, that then I may cease to bee at all.   2280
The Queene onely replied in Spanish, Dios lo sabe,
that is, God knoweth it, and so turning aside, left
her to bee conveyed to her former custody.

King Philip having privately over-heard the
Conference, was now fully settled in a good opinion
of her loyalty; hee, well perceiving the inveterate
malice of her Adversaries, and her extraordinary
patience in such a trial, did forthwith take order
for her deliverance. She in the interim remayned

very solitary, not knowing what the event would be;   2290

not one word of comfort could she imagine to have

proceeded from her Sister, yet, after long

expectation in this deluge of sorrows, a dove

appeared with an olive branch in her mouth. Within

seven dayes after, by the intercession of som eminent

friends, she was discharged of her keeper Sir Henry

Beningfield, yet so that Sir Thomas Pope one of her

Majesties privy Councell and Mr. Gage her Gentleman

usher were made superintendents over her. The change

was howsoever most happy; she was now in libera   2300

custodia, under the hands of her loving friends with

whom shee went downe into the Country, and there

spent the Remaynder of her Sisters raigne.

The bishop of Winchester and others of his

faction look'd blacke in the mouth to see all their

plots discovered, all their devices frustrate, yet

rather then they would give off, they would play at

small game; because they could not touch the Lady

Elizabeth, they would have a fling at her household,

and at those who were neerest unto her person. A   2310

warrant was sent downe for no lesse then foure of her

Gentlewomen at one time, which the Lady no sooner

heard of, but said, they will fetch away all in time.

But not long after, it so pleased God, that <u>Gardiner</u> himselfe was fetched away to give account for his actions; howsoever his death was the cause why she lived in lesse feare and more quietnesse.

Stephen <u>Gardiner</u>, Bishop of <u>Winchester</u>, hath had a long and tedious part in the troubles of the Lady <u>Elizabeth</u>; not one Scene of all her Tragicall Story   2320 but he hath had a share in it. It will not I hope bee therefore impertinent to write a line or two of his <u>Exit</u>, wherin I will wade no further then the warrant of sufficient Authority shall direct me:

The same day that those two bright shining lamps, Bishop <u>Ridley</u> and Master <u>Latimer</u> were extinguished at <u>Oxford</u>, <u>Gardiner</u> had invited the Duke of <u>Norfolke</u> and others to dinner, but caused the good old <u>Duke</u> to stay for it till about 3 or 4 a clock in the afternoone, being, as it should seem, not disposed to   2330 dine, till he had heard that fire was put to the two good Martyrs: he would not feede his own body, till theirs were quite consumed. At length came in a servant betwixt 3 and 4 and informed him of the certainty thereof. He no sooner understood it, but came out with great joy to the <u>Duke</u>, and said, <u>Come now let us goe to dinner</u>. The meat was served in, he

fell merrily aboard; but before the second messe came
in, he fell sick at the table and was immediatly
removed thence to bed, where he remayned full 15   2340
dayes in such anguish and torments that he could not
voyd what he had received, either by urine or
otherwise. Lying in this extremity, Doctor Day
Bishop of Chichester came to visite and comfort him
with words of Gods promise, and free Justification in
the bloud of Christ Jesus; which he no sooner heard,
but he answered thus: What my Lord, will you open
that gap now? Then farewell all together; to me and
such other in my case, you may speak it; but open
that Cazement once to the people, then farewell all   2350
together. More hee would have spoke, but his tongue
being so swell'd with the inflammation of his body he
became speechlesse and soone after died.

After the death of Gardiner, one or other of the
good Ladies Adversaries dropt away, insomuch, that by
little and little her dangers decreased, feares
diminished, and hope of comfort as out of a thick
cloud beganne to appeare. She spent the remaynder of
her Sisters reigne in thankes-giving, and prayses
unto God who had thus mercifully preserved her.   2360

The time of Queene Maries reckoning being come,

rumours were spred abroad that shee was already
delivered of a sonne, yea and such a one, as it was
then suspected, was readily prepared, whereof King
Philip being informed, and scorning that by any such
Impostory a counterfeit brood should be the heyre of
all his Kingdomes, would not depart the Chamber all
the time of her travell, by which meanes the Plot
tooke no effect; howsoever, the rumour of this young
Heyre made the Bells ring merily in London, and   2370
spread it selfe as farre as Antwerpe, where it was
entertained with great triumphs both on Land and Sea,
towards which charge an hundred Pistolets were
conferr'd on the Officers by the Lady Regent. But
the newes on their side was too good to bee true,
their joyfull acclamations too extreame to continue,
their Haleluiahs were instantly turn'd to Lachrymae;
the report proved but poin'd, and turned the Vane
presently into another poynt. It was after knowne to
all their greefes, that shee never had conceived, or   2380
ever was likely so to do; some gave out that shee was
with Child, but miscarried; some, that she had a
Timpany; others, that such a thing was rumour'd onely
for policy. But the truth is, King Philip seeing
himselfe frustrate of his expected Issue, and

perceiving such shuffling and cutting amongst them,
not long after took his leave of the Queene, to
visite his Father the Emperour, and take possession
of the Low-Countreys; his departure was very grievous
unto her, but (as most are of opinion) hee did but
little affect her.   2390

    King Philip stayed beyond Seas a full yeare and
six months. During his abode there, the Statists of
that time lost not the least opportunity to
extinguish, if it might bee possible, that Cause of
God, that hereticall faction, as they termed it. How
many deere Saints of God (during the Kings absence in
the space of 18 months) mounted up with Elias in a
fiery Chariot to Heaven? The fire was then at the
hottest, the flames were then at the highest, and the   2400
Lady Elizabeth, though peaceably seated in the
Countrey with her loving friends, yet was much
daunted with the fearefull apprehension of such
extremities. She feared the more, because shee knew
that such as were adverse unto her, would, like the
Divell, worke upon the weakenesse of her Sisters
frailety; they would leape over the hedge where it is
the lowest; and that now the absence of King Philip
beyond the seas was the only opportunity for the

advancement of their intended designes. But King   2410

Philips returne into England, not long after, proved

the happy resolution of all her feareful

apprehensions. Her life was a continuall warfare,

like a ship in the middst of an Irish Sea, where

nothing can be expected but troublesome stormes and

tempestuous waves, and certainly it will appeare,

that those perillous occurences shee met withall in

the foure yeeres of her Ante-Regnum during the

principality of her Sister, will way downe the

ballance, being poys'd with those severall Treasons   2420

which threatned her Majesty, being an absolute

Princesse. Then her opposites were aliens, now

natives (It was thou o my friend, &c); then forraigne

Kings sought to invade her, now a moderne Queene

strives to entrap her; they strangers, this a Sister;

she lived then at liberty without their jurisdiction,

now a prisoner captivated to an incensed Sisters

indignation; she was then attended by her Nobility,

and grave Counsellors, shee hath now not any to

converse with, but keepers and Gaolers. But that God   2430

wherein she still trusted, first, let her see her

desire upon her Adversaries, then in a good old age

gathered her to himselfe, freed her from the

opposition of the one, and the decease of Queen <u>Mary</u>
her Sister, set a period to the malice of the other.

    <u>Cardinall</u> <u>Poole</u> with the rest of that surviving
faction, seeing things thus retrograde to their
desires, perceiving the discontents of the Queene,
and that but a few sands were left in the glasse of
her time, they, <u>Nebuchadnezzar-like</u>, heated the oven   2440
of their persecution seaven times hotter then before.
For having already burned five Bishops, twenty one
Doctors, eight Gentlemen, eighty foure Artificers, an
hundreth Husbandmen, Servants, and labourers, twenty
sixe wives, twenty Widows, nine Virgins, two boyes,
two Infants, the one whipped to death, the other
sprange out of it's Mothers wombe being at the stake,
and was cruelly cast into fire againe; Sixty foure
persecuted, whereof seven whipped to death, 16 dyed
in prison and were buried in Dung-hils, many in   2450
Captivity abroad, leaving all they had, only for
conscience sake.

<u>Quis talia fando</u>,

<u>temperet a lachrimis</u>?

    Yet did not their fury cease here; they filled
the cup up to the brim. Perceiving the heat of those
fires beginne to slake and wanting fuell to encrease

the flames, they consulted to burne the bones of
those which had beene long since expired. They
digged up the bones of <u>Martyn</u> <u>Bucer</u> and <u>Paulus</u>   2460
<u>Phagius</u> long since buried, the one at Saint <u>Maries</u>,
the other at Saint <u>Michaels</u> in <u>Cambridge</u>, and with
great Pontificall State first degraded them, then
committed them to the secular power, afterward to the
fire; and lest the one Universitie should mock the
other, they tooke up the bones of <u>Peter</u> <u>Martirs</u> wife
formerly interr'd at <u>Oxford</u>, and buried them in a
stinking dunghill. Nay, in this fury, the bones of
<u>King</u> <u>Henry</u> the eight, and <u>Edward</u> the sixth, hardly
scaped free. Now they thought all sure, that the   2470
hereticall faction (as they termed it) were with
these bones utterly extinguished, but whilst they
thus solace themselves in the supposed victory of
Gods Saints, even then did the handwriting appeare
upon the wall against them. Newes came over that
<u>Calice</u> in France, a towne of great import, was
recovered by the <u>French</u>, having belonged to the
Crowne of <u>England</u> two hundred and eleven yeeres, and
herin the losse of <u>Calice</u> was most memorable. It was
first won by <u>Edward</u> the third, being the eleventh   2480
King from <u>William</u> the <u>Conquerour</u>, and lost againe by

Mary, being the eleventh from Edward, in 8 dayes.
The Queene took the losse to heart; the people
beganne to murmure, some imputing the losse unto the
neglect of the Clergy, who then sate at the helme of
state, others whispered that it was a just Judgement
of God for the abundance of bloud already spilt and
broyled in the land. In the interim, those of the
faction strive to allay the heat of this
distemperature both in Prince and People, by   2490
extenuation of the losse, saying, that it was a Towne
of none such consequence, but rather of greater
inconvenience then they were aware of, that it was
onely a refuge for runnagate hereticks, and
consequently, that no true Romane Catholik ought to
deplore, but rather rejoyce at the dammage.

At Regina gravi

iamdudum saucia cura

Vulnus alit venis.------

Howsoever the Queene being struck to the heart,   2500
the wound became uncurable; then they call'd a
Parliament. Many large profers were made for the
recovery of Calice wherin the clergy did exceed, yet
all this would not do; Calice still stuck in the
Queenes stomack. She went up and downe mourning and

sighing all the day long, which being asked her by
some, what was the reason thereof, whether King
Philips departure were the occasion? No said she,
The losse of Calice is written in my heart, and there
may be reade the occasion of my griefe, when after   2510
death my body shall bee opened. Her conceptions at
length fayling, great dearth in the land raigning,
much harme done by thunders on shoare, and by fire on
her Royall Fleete at Sea, home troubles, forraigne
losses, King Philips unkindnesse, these with other
discontentments brought her to a burning feaver, of
which she died at Saint James nere Westminster, on
the 17th of November being Thursday, Anno 1558, and
lyes buried in a chappell in Saint Peters
Westminster, without any monument or remembrance at   2520
all.

Queene Mary was well inclined of her selfe; had
not the blind zeale of her Religion, and authority of
the clergy overswayd her, the flames of their
consuming fire had not mounted so high as heaven,
there to solicite for vengeance. It is observed that
her raigne was the shortest of all Kings since the
conquest (Richard the third only excepted) and that
more christian blood was spilt in her short time,

then had beene in case of Religion in any Kings raign   2530
whatsoever, since King <u>Lucius</u>, the first establisher
of Christianity in <u>England</u>, and God grant the like
may never be seene againe, Amen.

The Cloud thus set, that wished Sunne appeared in
our horizon like a fresh spring after a stormy
winter. The Parliament then sitting at <u>Westminster</u>,
newes was brought that the Queen was deceased; the
soddainnesse of the news struck the house into
amazment.

Some look'd backward to the dead Queene, others   2540
looked forward to the surviving Princesse, but at
last they pitch'd upon the proclamation of the Lady
<u>Elizabeth</u>, which was accordingly performed the same
day, in the 24th yeere, 2 month and 10 day of her
age, at what time she remooved from <u>Hatfield</u> to the
<u>Charterhouse</u>. From thence she was royally attended
to the <u>Tower</u> of <u>London</u>, and the 24 of the same month
passed with great state through the City to
<u>Westminster</u>.

On the foure and twentieth of <u>November</u>, Queen   2550
<u>Elizabeth</u> set forward from the <u>Tower</u>, to passe thorow
the City to <u>Westminster</u>, but considering that after
so long restraint she was now exalted from misery to

Majesty, from a Prisoner to a Princesse, before shee would suffer herself to be mounted in her Chariot, shee very devoutely lifted up Her Handes and Eyes to Heaven, uttering these words:

O Lord Almighty and ever-living God, I give thee most humble and hearty thankes, that thou hast beene so mercifull unto mee, as to spare mee to see this 2560 joyfull and blessed Day; and I acknowledge that thou hast dealt as graciously and wonderfully with me, as thou didst with thy true and faithfull Servant, Daniel thy Prophet, whom thou delivered'st out of the Lyons Denne, from the crueltie of the greedy and raging Lyons: even so was I over-whelmed, and by thee delivered. To thee therefore onely bee thankes and honour and prayse for evermore. Amen.

Having made an end of her thankes-giving to God, shee put onwards through the City, where divers 2570 magnificent Pageants presented themselves to her view. The throng of people was extraordinary, their acclamations loud as thunder; many were the expressions of love tendred unto her, and by her as gratefully entertained as they were lovingly presented. To make a particular relation of the severall occurrences in that one dayes entertainment

would require above a dayes expression. I will onely
but point at some more remarkeable passages, wherein
shee shewed her selfe extraordinarily affected to her   2580
People.

She would many times cause her Charriot to stand,
that the people might have their full sight of her.
Amongst the severall speeches that were addressed
unto her from the Pageants, if at any time any word
did reflect upon her, a change of countenance was
observed in her; but a settled constancie to heare it
out; then her love and courtesie in giving the people
thankes. In Cornehill a Pageant presented it selfe,
called the Seate of worthy Governement, intimating   2590
their dutifull allegiance to her, with the generall
conceived hopes of her Princely Governement; the
Speech was no sooner delivered, but shee immediately
answered.

I have taken notice of your good meaning toward
mee, and will endeavour to Answere your severall
expectations.

Passing forward, another Pageant appeared,
representing the eight Beatitudes, every one applyed
to her in particular by the Speaker, the multitude   2600
crying out, Amen, Amen. But being come to the litle

Conduit in <u>Cheape</u>, shee perceived an offer of Love, and demanded what it might signifie? One told her <u>Grace</u> that there was placed <u>Time</u>; <u>Time</u>! (said shee) <u>and Time I praise my God hath brought me hither</u>. <u>But what is that other with the Booke</u>? Shee was resolved that it was <u>Truth</u>, the Daughter of <u>Time</u>, presenting the <u>Bible</u> in <u>English</u>, whereunto she answered, <u>I thanke the Citie for this guift above all the rest; it is a Booke which I will often and often read over</u>.   2610
Then she commanded Sir <u>John Perrot</u>, one of the Knights that held up the Canopie, to goe and receive the <u>Bible</u>; but being informed that it was to bee let downe unto her by a silken string shee commanded him to stay. In the <u>Interim</u> a <u>Purse</u> of gold was presented by the <u>Recorder</u> in the behalfe of the City, which shee received with her owne hands, and afterward gave attention to a speech delivered, making reply in the conclusion:

   <u>I thanke my Lord Mayor, his brethren the</u>   2620
<u>Aldermen, and all of you, and whereas your request is that I should continue your good Lady and Queene, be you assured that I will be as good unto you as ever Queene was yet unto her people</u>. <u>No will in me is wanting, neither doe I hope can there want any power</u>.

114

As for the priviledges and Charters of your City, I
will in discharge of my oath and affection, see them
safely and exactly maintained, and perswade your
selves that for the safety and quietnes of you all, I
will not spare, if need bee, to spend my blood in   2630
your behalfe. God blesse you all good people.

   As shee went along in Fleete-streete at St.
Dunstans Church, the children of Christ's Hospitall
sate there with the governours. Shee tooke great
delight in the object, and calling to minde that it
was her brothers foundation, shee expressed her selfe
very thankefull for the presentation of such a
charitable sight, saying: Wee are Orphans all; let me
enjoy your Prayers, and you shall be sure of my
assistance. As shee went through Temple-Barre, the   2640
Ordinance and Chambers of the Tower went off, the
report whereof gave much content: thus passed Shee
along to West-minster, royally attended with the
Nobility of the Kingdom, and was there Crowned, to
the joy of all true-hearted Christians.

             Est et quod Regnat causa
                  fuisse piam.
                   FINIS.

EMENDATIONS OF SUBSTANTIVES

7.   of the] 32; of the of the 31

17.   both cruell and] 32; om. 31

24.   he] 32; Her 31

44.   flee] 32; flye 31

44-45.   those words] 32; that 31

66.   Polypragmatists] 32; Polupragmatists 31

135.   enjoying] 32; enjoyning 31

144.   Prerogative] 32; Prerogatives 31

155.   as] 32; but --- 31

163.   Henry] 32; Edward 31

284.   whose] 32; whsoe 31

323.   Lord] 32; Lod 31

376.   to] 32; to to 31

401.   William] 32; Medlin 31

435.   Anna] 32; Iana 31

464.   necessarily] 32; nccessarily 31

532.   languages] 32; language, 31

555.   of] 32; om. 31

660.   as] 32; om. 31

675-76. convenient speed she] 32; convenient 31(u);
conveniẽce 31 (c)

680. Protector] 32; Pro-|Protector 31

765. Dominions] 32; Domini-|nions 31

775. they] 32; he 31

776. him] 32; them 31

895. Durham] 32; Duresme 31

928. although] 32; althoug 31

952. Although] 32; althought 31

983. and] 32; & --- 31

992. and] 32; where being 31

1170. removed] 32; remove 31

1197. it] 32; that --- 31

1227. of] 32; o 31

1279. retrahuntque sequamur] 32; retrahuntq sequemur 31

1296. brought] 32; brougt 31

1451. your] 32; her 31

1511. Lords] 32; Lord 31

1651. Crofts] 32; Acrofts 31

1654. Ashridge] 32; Abridge 31

1820. Gaoler.] 32; Goaler 31

1821. Gaoler]; Goaler 31

1821. but] 32; but but 31

1858. Erostratus] 41; Sostratus 31

1865. galled] 32; alled 31

1893. <u>Gaoler</u>]; <u>Goaler</u> 31

1955. <u>blessings</u>] 32; <u>blessngs</u> 31

1970. impell] 32; impells 31

1973. another] 32; a|nother 31

1989. flee] 32; flye 31

1990. Cup] 32; Cups 31

2010. Letters] 32; Lettets 31

2025. <u>hereafter</u>] 32; <u>hereafer</u> 31

2059. inciting] 32; in-|inciting 31

2130. at] 32; at at 31

2169. to] 32; <u>om</u>. 31

2235. <u>advantage of</u>] 32; --- <u>of of</u> 31

2286. perceiving] 32; perceived 31

2333. quite] 32; quit 31

2337. <u>let</u>] 32; <u>lets</u> 31

2344. <u>Chichester</u>] 32; <u>Winchester</u> 31

2360. God] 32; Gods 31

2417. perillous] 32; peillous 31

2430. Gaolers]; Goalers 31

2454. <u>temperet</u>] 32; <u>tempreet</u> 31

2461-62. the one . . . <u>Michaels</u>] 32 [<u>italic added</u>]; at Saint
                <u>Maries</u> 31

2515. these]; there 31

2515. other] 32; others 31

2518. November] 32; February 31

2561. acknowledge] 32; acknowlede 31

EMENDATIONS OF ACCIDENTALS

4. Tractate]; ---, 31+

7. minoritie),]; ---:)$_\wedge$ 31

12. Kinsman)] 32; ---:) 31

15. Friends,]; ---: 31

17. safety] H; ---, 31

18. adversaries. Which] 32; ---, which 31

21. enemies,]; ---; 31+

28-29. History. Be] 32; ---: [No ¶] Be 31

32. Monument] 32; ---, 31

34. him. What] 32; ---: what 31

35. appeared] 32; ---, 31

36. 1588,] 32; ---. 31

39. It] 32; [No ¶] --- 31

41. mee] 32; ---, 31

44. refuge] 32; ---, 31

50. present,] 32; ---; 31

53. THOMAS]; THO: 31

58. Candle,]; ---; 31+

91. intentions,]; ---; 31+

94.   thereunto. As] 32; ---, as 31

113.   7th,]; ---. 31

115.   Spaine. Shee] 32; ---, shee 31

119-20.   Death . . . Princes,] 32; (--- . . . ---) 31

120.   the] 32; The 31

122.   greatnesse),]; ---)ᴧ 31+

129.   performed.] 32; ---; 31

146.   incestuous. Some] 32; ---, some 31

148.   Clergy. But] 32; ---, but 31

150.   Conscience was]; ---, ---, 31

151.   Bayon,]; ---ᴧ 31+

173.   pleasures.] 32; ---: 31

174.   was,]; ---ᴧ 31+

194-95.   Point. The]; ---: the 31+

196.   Friers. The] 32; ---; the 31

197.   hand] 41; ---, 31

202.   cause:] 32; ---, 31

205-06.   King, . . . honored,] H; ---ᴧ . . . ---ᴧ 31

208.   speake.)]; ---ᴧ) 31

208.   But] 32; but 31

210.   September] 32; Sept. 31

210.   1532,] 32; ---. 31

214.   selfe] 41; ---, 31

218.   steps] H; ---, 31

223. <u>God</u>] 32; ---, 31

223. <u>power</u>] 41; ---, 31

224. <u>willeth</u>,]; ---; 31+

226. rest] H; ---, 31

226. utter,] 32; ---_∧ 31

228. 1533,] 32; ---. 31

230. <u>Bullein</u>,] 32; ---; 31

231. privately:] 32; ---, 31

236. traine. This] 32; ---, this 31

244. <u>Katharine</u>,] 32; ---_∧ 31

246. <u>Anne</u>,] 32; ---_∧ 31

247. honored.] 32; ---: 31

247. adored:] 32; ---_∧ 31

248. acclamations] 32; ---, 31

252. 3 and 4]; 3o --- 4% 31

253. who,]; ---_∧ 31+

260. <u>Greenewich</u>. The]; ---, the 31+

264. witnesses] 32; ---, 31

264. were]; ---, 31+

281. observeth)] 32; ---, 31

285. succession. Wherby] 32; ---, wherby 31

288. Royall]; ---, 31+

288. <u>Anne</u>.] 32; ---: 31

298. was,] H; ---_∧ 31

308. others. They] 32; ---, they 31

310. ranne]; ---, 31+

312. delighted;]; ---: 31+

316. Westminster,] 32; Westmin. 31

319. thereof.] 32; ---: 31

320. quiet,] 32; ---; 31

321.. perceived;]; ---, 31

339. Tower. At] 32; ---, at 31

340. was]; ---, 31+

344-45. message. But]; ---, but 31

347. confident] H; ---, 31

349. it;]; ---, 31

350. behaviour] 32; ---, 31

353. telling her]; --- ---, 31+

353. command]; ---, 31+

355. remaine] 32; ---, 31

355-56. pleasure. To] 32; ---, to 31

356. answered]; ---, 31+

359. obeyed. So] 32; ---: so 31

364. Tower. The]; ---: the 31+

364. Lieutenant] 32; Luietenant 31

369. crime]; ---, 31+

369. me. Then] 32; ---: then 31

370. you] H; ---, 31

372. mee;]; ---, 31

375. Tower. The]; ---; the 31+

383. England. The] 32; ---, the 31

386. discretion]; ---, 31+

388. whatsoever.] 32; ---: 31

390. her, the]; ---; The 31

394. pleasure.] 32; ---; 31

396. Aunt]; ---, 31

407. after,] H; ---ᴧ 31

410. London,] 32; ---ᴧ 31

411. Spectators. Her] 32; ---, her 31

412. these:]; ---, 31+

415. me. As] 32; ---, as 31

416. speak;] H; ---, 31

420. Soule. Next]; ---; next 31+

422. lives,]; ---; 31+

425. bosome;]; ---, 31

446. servants. The] 32; ---, the 31

447. her.] 32; ---; 31

453. crossed;]; ---, 31

468. children. Heereupon] 32; ---; heereupon 31

477. daughters;] 32; ---, 31

484. Coxe] H; ---, 31

485. Cheeke. As] 32; ---, as 31

487. Lady.] 32; ---, 31

491. Documents. The] 32; ---, the 31

501. wombe. They] 32; ---, they 31

504. correspondencie:] 32; ---, 31

509. breake. Their] 32; ---, their 31

512. schooling. Besides] 32; ---, besides 31

523. Princes.] 32; ---; 31

527. needle.] 32; ---; 31

528. employment.] 32; ---, 31

529. actions.] 32; ---, 31

529. Principium:] 32; ---, 31

530. them;] 32; ---, 31

532. Arts. Most] 32; ---, most 31

533. theirs.] 32; ---, 31

544. willingnesse] 32; ---, 31

549. life;]; ---, 31

553. them. How] 32; ---: how 31

563. wither. The] 32; ---, the 31

578. them.] 32; ---; 31

582. pleasure.] 32; ---: 31

585. both,] 32; ---ˏ 31

593. King,] H; ---ˏ 31

598. Sonne;]; ---, 31

600. following] 32; ---, 31

604. yeares. On] 32; ---, on 31

612. King;] 32; ---, 31

616. State. There] 32; ---, there 31

618. them;]; ---, 31

620. Soveraigne.] 32; ---; 31

622. Sister;]; ---, 31

627. Countrey;]; ---, 31

636. them.] 32; ---, 31

639. Country,] 32; ---ᴧ 31

642. health. Shee] 32; ---, shee 31

643-44. Governesse. Scarce] 32; ---: scarce 31

649. he,]; ---ᴧ 31

651. repulses]; ---, 31+

655. Countrey. For] 32; ---; for 31

664. Lady,] 32; L. 31

669. Marriage] H; ---, 31

670. retyred.] 32; ---; 31

673. Residence] 32; ---, 31

679. Seymour.] 32; ---, 31

681. these]; These 31+

687. Gray,] 32; ---ᴧ 31

697. it] 32; ---, 31

702. husband). She] 32; ---)ᴧ she 31

704. place. Both] 32; ---, both 31

706. other. The] 32; ---, the 31

708. Protector. The] 32; ---, the 31

709. women;]; ---, 31

711. secretly.]; ---; 31

712. parts;]; ---, 31+

718. 20,] H; ---. 31

722. other. In] 32; ---: in 31

722. February] 41; Febr. 31

724-25. Councell. Many]; ---, many 31

729. released. This] 32; ---, this 31

751. Suffolke.] 32; ---: 31

754. Jane.] 32; ---; 31

757. Westminster. He] 32; ---, he 31

763. projected.] 32; ---; 31

768. people.] 32; ---: 31

772. tongue. Hee] 32; ---: hee 31

774. admiration.] 32; ---; 31

777. study.] 32; ---; 31

778. unguem;]; ---, 31

783. key. Hee] 32; ---; hee 31

785. Poore. Hee] 32; ---, hee 31

787. Commonweale. Hee] 32; ---; hee 31

795. Latine. Hee] 32; ---; hee 31

797. age;] H; ---, 31

797-805. St.] H; S. 31

806. <u>speare</u>.] 32; ---; 31

814. Religiously. Being] 32; ---, being 31

819. manner:]; ---. 31

821. <u>chosen</u>;]; ---: 31+

822. <u>done</u>.]; ---: 31+

824. <u>thee</u>;]; ---: 31+

830. <u>sake</u>. To]; ---: to 31+

831. added:]; ---; 31+

834. Nose-gay;]; ---: 31+

838. <u>Jane</u>]; ---, 31+

841. Nobility. Hereupon] 32; ---; hereupon 31

844. inheritance;]; ---: 31

849. <u>Mary</u>. The] 32; ---: the 31

853. him. The]; ---, the 31+

854. him; so] 32; ---, --- 31

858. Market-place. Yet.] 32; ---, yet 31

861. head.] 32; ---; 31

862. <u>Northumberland</u>.] 32; ---: 31

864. <u>Northumberland</u>,] 32; <u>Northumb</u>. 31

866. they] 32; They 31

869. 8th,] 32; ---. 31

873. Ruines.] 32; ---, 31

873. <u>Mary</u>,] 32; ---ᴧ 31

878. <u>Elizabeth</u>,] H; ---ᴧ 31

882. to. But] 32; ---, but 31

886. <u>omnes</u>;] 32; ---, 31

890. <u>Gardiner</u>. Soone] 32; ---; soone 31

890. after,] H; ---ᴧ 31

891. <u>Edward</u>]; ---, 31+

893. out;] 32; ---, 31

894. confin'd;] 32; confind', 31

895. excluded;] 32; ---, 31

895. <u>Durham</u>;]; ---, 31+

897. <u>Fleete</u>;] 32; ---, 31

897. <u>Exeter</u>,] 32; ---; 31

898. cashier'd.] 32; ---; 31

908. <u>West-minster</u>.] 32; ---; 31

909. <u>Elizabeth</u>,] 32; ---ᴧ 31

916. <u>Gardiner</u>,] H; ---ᴧ 31

917. <u>Winchester</u>]; ---, 31+

918. <u>Tower</u>).] 32; ---)ᴧ 31

919. Coronation. Five] 32; ---; five 31

933. <u>will</u>.] 32; ---: 31

937. <u>estate</u>;]; ---: 31+

941. <u>innocent</u>.] 32; ---: 31

943. <u>know</u>] 32; ---) 31

943. <u>enough</u>)] 32; ---ᴧ 31

944. <u>assayed</u>,]; ---; 31+

946. <u>Lawes</u>;]; ---: 31+

949. <u>heart</u>.] 32; ---: 31

951-52. <u>hand</u>. <u>Although</u>] 32; ---, <u>althought</u> 31

965. father. Much] 32; ---; much 31

966. <u>Jane</u>. The] 32; ---, the 31

970. father,] 32; ---_∧ 31

974. <u>Jane</u>.] 32; ---: 31

979. law;]; ---: 31

980. 1554,] 32; ---. 31

985. death.] 32; ---: 31

989. terrour]; ---, 31+

991. death. Being] 32; ---; being 31

992. Scaffold,] 32; ---_∧ 31

995. <u>same</u>. <u>My</u>] 32; ---; <u>my</u> 31

998. <u>those</u>]; ---, 31+

1004. <u>all</u>] 32; ---; 31

1004. <u>day</u>.] 32; ---: 31

1005. Booke,] 32; ---_∧ 31

1005. thus:]; ---, 31

1009. <u>Christ</u>.] 32; ---; 31

1013. <u>sinnes</u>;]; ---, 31

1022. <u>Tower</u>. Beginning] 32; ---; beginning 31

1027. attires.] 32; ---: 31

1030. _canst_. Then] 32; ———; then 31

1032. He] 32; he 31

1032. _Madame_. Then] 32; ———; then 31

1035. Then] H; then 31

1037. _spirit_. The] 32; ———, the 31

1044. life.] 32; ———ʌ 31

1049. person.] 32; ———: 31

1050. vertues] 32; ———, 31

1052. praecellent:] 32; ———, 31

1054. Execution. Shee] 32; ———, shee 31

1055. unambitious]; ———, 31+

1057. teares. Whilst] 32; ———; whilst 31

1061. _possint_:] 32; ———, 31

1065. _incline_:] 32; ———, 31

1068. thus:]; ———. 31

1075. _intention_.]; ———, 31

1093. Third. As] 32; ———; as 31

1100. fidelity;]; ———, 31

1105. _London_] 32; ———, 31

1108. _February_] 32; _Feb_. 31

1113. next.] 32; ———: 31

1115. Countrey. The] 32; ———; the 31

1119. understanding] 32; ———, 31

1121. broken,] 32; ———ʌ 31

1122. storme,] 32; ---, 31

1125. Ours] 32; ---, 31

1128. encounters. Hee] 32; ---; hee 31

1129. Holy-dayes;] 32; ---, 31

1132. him.] 32; ---; 31

1133. the Troubles]; The --- 31

1134. Comment.] 32; ---; 31

1137. There] H; there 31

1140-41. <u>Winchester</u>, . . . Agent,] 32; ---, . . . ---, 31

1146. <u>et</u>] H; <u>&</u> 31

1149. <u>Gardiner</u>,] H; ---, 31

1156. enterprise. Sir] 32; ---, (--- 31

1159. same,] 32; ---) 31

1161. Religion. Here] 32; ---, here 31

1163. sure;] 32; ---, 31

1163. at] 41; ---, 31

1167. indignation;] 32; ---, 31

1169. sojourned,] 32; ---, 31

1173. <u>Williams</u>,] H; ---, 31

1180. death. The]; ---, the 31+

1181. on;]; ---, 31

1187. amazement. But] 32; ---; but 31

1190. House]; ---, 31

1192. <u>Ashley</u>,] 32; ---, 31

1195. Queene. The] 32; ---: the 31

1197. againe]; ---, 31

1197. (it] 32; ˄--- 31

1198. sicke)] 32; ---, 31

1201. morning. But] 32; ---, but 31

1203. staires]; ---, 31+

1206. intrusion. They] 32; ---; they 31

1206. They,] H; they˄ 31

1207. speech] 32; ---, 31

1208. the] 32; The 31

1211. especially]; ---, 31+

1214. Westminster. To] 32; ---; to 31

1221. hast. But] 32; ---, but 31

1224. shee. Hereupon] 32; ---, hereupon 31

1231. mortall. Their] 32; ---: their 31

1244. good-night. They] 32; ---; they 31

1245. respect] 32; ---, 31

1246. first] 32; ---, 31

1250. London. The] 32; ---, the 31

1259. enemies. In] 32; ---, in 31

1260. night;]; ---, 31

1263-64. Albones. From] 32; ---; from 31

1274. Lodging. Shee] 32; ---; shee 31

1279. retrahuntque]; retrahuntq; 31

1283. fortune. She] 32; ---; she 31

1286. expelled. Thus] 32; ---, thus 31

1294. her. Being] 32; ---; being 31

1297. on.] 32; ---: 31

1303. proceedings. For]; ---; for 31

1314-15. selfe? After] 32; ---, after 31

1318. circumstance]; ---, 31+

1322. Majestie. Wherunto] 32; ---: wherunto 31

1326. councell.] 32; ---; 31

1328. pleasure. They] 32; ---; they 31

1331. selfe]; ---, 31+

1335. Columns.] 32; ---; 31

1345. <u>Tower</u>. The] 32; ---, the 31

1345. of <u>Tower</u>] 32; --- ---, 31

1348. visage. Shee] 32; ---, shee 31

1348. words:] H; ---. 31

1350. <u>If</u>] 32; <u>if</u> 31

1364. replyed]; ---, 31+

1366. behalfe;]; ---, 31

1369. unalterable. When] 32; ---, when 31

1369. When,] H; when_∧ 31

1369. pause, well,] 32; ---; ---_∧ 31

1374. <u>wisedome</u>;]; ---, 31

1380. <u>straightned</u>;]; ---, 31

1381. <u>last</u>. <u>Whilst</u>]; ---, <u>whilst</u> 31

1383. <u>issue</u>:] 32; ---, 31

1384. <u>Comforter</u>. And] 32; ---; and 31

1389. for,] 32; ---ᴧ 31

1390. them] 32; ---, 31

1390. omit),]; ---)ᴧ 31+

1390. the] 32; The 31

1391. body. Upon] 32; ---, upon 31

1396. granted. Then] 32; ---; then 31

1398. admit. But] 32; ---: but 31

1400. said]; ---, 31+

1405. writing]; ---, 31+

1408. quality),]; ---)ᴧ 31+

1408. spent. Then] 32; ---, then 31

1411. midnight. The] 32; ---, the 31

1413. rescued. Therefore] 32; ---, therefore 31

1417. presently. Whereunto] 32; ---, whereunto 31

1418. <u>done</u>. <u>Since</u>]; ---, <u>since</u> 31

1420. <u>contented</u>. Passing] 32; ---; passing 31

1423. thus:]; ---, 31+

1425. <u>England</u>.] 32; ---: 31

1425. <u>why</u>,] H; ---ᴧ 31

1427. <u>The</u>]; <u>the</u> 31+

1431. danger. The] 32; ---, the 31

1438. Traytors. Loath] 32; ---; loath 31

1441. State;]; ---: 31+

1442. convoy,] 32; ---; 31

1444. words:] H; ---. 31

1444. God,] 32; ---; 31

1445. confidence:] 32; ---, 31

1450. you. As] 32; ---; as 31

1451. attending]; ---, 31+

1458. complaine. The] 32; ---: the 31

1461. brought. Then] 32; ---; then 31

1463. raine;]; ---, 31

1464. usage.] 32; ---; 31

1466. it.] 32; ---: 31

1467. Bridges,] 32; ---ᴧ 31

1474. owne]; ---, 31+

1482-83. her. Whereunto] 32; ---, whereunto 31

1484. unknowne] 32; ---, 31

1486. unknowne] 32; ---, 31

1486-87. temptation. This] 32; ---: this 31

1489. sufficiencie. Death] 32; ---, death 31

1491. us. But] 32; ---: but 31

1495. encouragement.] 32; ---; 31

1496. Grace;]; ---, 31

1497. neede. Though] 32; ---, though 31

1500. confident.]; ---, 31+

1501. Thou]; thou 31+

1505. performed. But] 32; ---; but 31

1509. beare;]; ---, 31

1511. answerable. The] 32; ---: the 31

1514. Gardiner,]; ---ᴧ 31+

1522. danger. Shee] 32; ---, shee 31

1523. downe,] 32; ---ᴧ 31

1524. indignity:] 32; ---, 31

1525. storme. The] 32; ---; the 31

1527. meanes;]; ---, 31

1532. Elizabeth] 32; ---: 31

1532. (all] 32; ᴧAll 31

1536. custody] 32; ---, 31

1536. Tower),]; ---ᴧ, 31

1539. 1554,] 32; ---. 31

1542. Nobility. At] 32; ---: at 31

1544. Legge. Before] 32; ---; before 31

1547. Voyage. Having] 32; ---: having 31

1559. Lodgings. Lowd] 32; ---; lowd 31

1560. the Bishop] 32; The --- 31

1566-67. Quire. Perceiving] 32; ---, perceiving 31

1571. seconded. That] 32; ---, that 31

1573. him. All] 32; ---; all 31

1577. way. Shee]; ---, shee 31

1578. lovingly. They]; ---, they 31

1582. following,] H; ---ᴧ 31

1586. <u>English</u>. Hee] 32; ---: hee 31

1587. Cloath;] 32; ---, 31

1588. men. At] 32; ---; at 31

1589. plaid. The] 32; ---; the 31

1593. houre. Hee] 32; ---, hee 31

1597. <u>James</u> day,] 32; ---, ---ᴧ 31

1598. 25,] 32; ---. 31

1601. Gard]; ---, 31+

1604. <u>Pembrooke</u>. Being] 32; ---, being 31

1605. Altar] 32; ---, 31

1607. thought] 32; ---, 31

1613. <u>English</u>;]; ---, 31

1615. Stone. The] 32; ---: the 31

1616. together;] 32; ---, 31

1627. <u>Tirroll</u>,]; ---: 31+

1636. <u>Southwarke</u>;] 32; ---, 31

1638. <u>West-minster</u>. Great] 32; ---; great 31

1644. <u>Tower</u>,] 32; ---; 31

1645. death. It] 32; ---; it 31

1648. throat.] 32; ---: 31

1654. privately]; ---, 31+

1655. Castle.] 32; ---ᴧ 31

1658. House;]; ---: 31

1661. mee. If] 32; ---; if 31

1664. offendors. As] 32; ---: as 31

1665. James] 32; Ja. 31

1669. Subject. But] 32; ---; but 31

1669-70. purpose, my Lords? Might] 32; ---ᴧ (--- ---)
          might 31

1672. Earle]; E. 31

1674. troubled] 32; ---, 31

1675. moment. Well] 32; ---; well 31

1677. me] 32; ---, 31

1682. her] 41; ---, 31

1686. objected,]; ---; 31+

1687. Prisoner. The]; ---, the 31

1692. ordered,] H; ---; 31

1693. imprisonment]; ---, 31+

1694. motion. Neither] 32; ---; neither 31

1696. hers. Violent] 32; ---; violent 31

1697. innocence;]; ---, 31+

1709. execution.] 32; ---; 31

1710. engine,]; ---; 31+

1713. Queen. Shee] 32; ---, shee 31

1719. after, . . . May,] H; ---ᴧ . . . ---ᴧ 31

1731. them. These] 32; ---; these 31

1735. seene,] 32; ---; 31

1738. Hee] 32; hee 31

1740. remaining;]; ---: 31

1744. Answer] 32; answer 31

1745. that] 32; ---, 31

1745. man] 32; ---, 31

1753. comfort;]; ---, 31

1759. Lodgings,] H; ---; 31

1761. by-]; ---‸ 31+

1761. out-houses;]; ---, 31

1765. morning. Wherewith] 32; ---; wherewith 31

1768. grace. If] 32; ---, if 31

1770. still;]; ---, 31

1773. him. Bee] 32; ---; bee 31

1774. dejected;] 32; ---, 31

1775. morning. Shee] 32; ---; shee 31

1776. added:]; ---; 31+

1779-80. overpast. Hereupon] 32; ---: hereupon 31

1783. conceived. Comming] 32; ---; comming 31

1786. him]; ---, 31+

1791. rescue.] 32; ---: 31

1795. defence. So] 32; ---: so 31

1798. people,]; ---‸ 31+

1803. afforded. The] 32; ---, the 31

1809. Traytors,] 32; ---ᴧ 31

1811. noone] 32; ---, 31

1812. stocks. The] 32; ---; the 31

1816. <u>bablings</u>. <u>Besides</u>]; ---, <u>besides</u> 31

1820. Gaoler. The] 32; Goaler; the 31

1825. <u>thinkes</u>] 32; ---, 31

1826. <u>together</u>. <u>Let</u>]; ---; <u>let</u> 31+

1827. Commission;] 32; ---, 31

1830. servants,]; ---ᴧ 31+

1834. carryed. To] 32; ---, to 31

1839. Grace. The] 32; ---; the 31

1844. them]; ---, 31+

1849. after-clappes. Whereunto] 32; ---: whereunto 31

1853. house.] 32; ---: 31

1863. behaviour. That] 32; ---; that 31

1865. galled,] 32; ---ᴧ 31

1867. him,] 41; ---; 31

1873. <u>Tower</u>. Here] 32; ---, here 31

1876. Soldiers. Besides,] 32; ---, besidesᴧ 31

1884. severity. In] 32; ---, in 31

1890-91. keyes. Whereupon] 32; ---, whereupon 31

1891. him: <u>Why</u>,]; ---; ---; 31

1898. other. Not] 32; ---, not 31

1899. instruction:] 41; ---, 31

1901. selfe. Then]; ---; then 31

1908. leaves,]; ---; 31+

1911. branches;]; ---, 31

1914-15. People. Then] 32; ---; then 31

1919. soyle;] 32; ---, 31

1924. more. Shee] 32; ---, shee 31

1930. extinguished. Shee] 32; ---; shee 31

1931. tryall. The]; ---; the 31

1932-33. Saints. There] 32; ---, there 31

1935-36. Kingdome. What] 32; ---; what 31

1950. sindged.] 32; ---: 31

1956. Then] 32; then 31

1957. pray:] H; ---. 31

1961. me.] 32; ---; 31

1966. hand.]; ---, 31

1968. thee. The] 32; ---; the 31

1970. complaine. If] 41; ---; if 31

1977. _Captive_. Hast] 32; ---; hast 31

1979. Will]; will 31+

1980. Will]; will 31+

1988. _Jesus_). There]; ---)ᴧ there 31

1990. sorrow. Whatsoever] 32; ---; whatsoever 31

1992. me. Helpe] 32; ---; helpe 31

1993. raised;] H; ---, 31

1994. illuminated;] H; ---, 31

1995. exalted;] H; ---, 31

1999. her. Shee]; ---, shee 31

2002. Philosophy. But] 32; ---; but 31

2006. permitted.] 32; ---; 31

2011. pleasure. But] 32; ---; but 31

2012. said] 32; ---, 31

2012. Court.] H; ---: 31

2013. them;]; ---, 31+

2015. therin. Wherunto] 32; ---: wherunto 31

2016. Queene;] 32; ---, 31

2021. were.] 32; ---, 31

2022. contrary;] H; ---, 31

2023. it. Her] 32; ---; her 31

2026. mee. Then] 32; ---: then 31

2031. Highnesse.] 32; ---: 31

2036. maintaine.] 32; ---; 31

2039-40. you. Being] 32; ---: being 31

2045. Queene.] 32; ---; 31

2046. heart. Then] 32; ---; then 31

2049-50. Dr . . . Dr] H; D . . . D 31

2050. her. Being] 32; ---: being 31

2059. telling her] 32; --- ---, 31

2064. Queene,]; Qu. 31

2066. inlargement. The] 32; ---; the 31

2067. manner:]; ---, 31+

2069. <u>life</u>.] 32; ---; 31

2071. <u>all</u>;] 41; ---, 31

2072. <u>me</u>. <u>My</u>]; ---; <u>my</u> 31+

2075. <u>happy</u>;]; ---, 31

2078. party,] 32; ---_∧ 31

2082. ends. Great] 32; ---; great 31

2083. her. The] 32; ---, the 31

2087. abroad. But] 32; ---, but 31

2088. one:]; ---, 31

2090. shoulders;]; ---: 31+

2097-98. <u>mischiefe</u>. And] 32; ---; and 31

2102. effected.] 32; ---; 31

2105. good. During] 32; ---, during 31

2117. Queene]; Queeene 31

2121. disappointed. These] 32; ---: these 31

2123. increasing,] H; ---; 31

2135. Churches.]; ---; 31

2138. <u>Elizabeth</u>;]; ---, 31

2142. Conscience] 32; ---, 31

2144. strangers. Hee] 32; ---; hee 31

2156. after,] 32; ---_∧ 31

2158. <u>Henry</u>] 32; <u>Hen</u>: 31

2160. way. As] 32; ---; as 31

2162. her;] 32; ---, 31

2167. unready. The] 32; ---, the 31

2170. could. That] 32; ---, that 31

2173. <u>George</u>. Divers]; ---, divers 31+

2174. her,]; ---: 31+

2177. other. The] 32; ---; the 31

2180-81. ward. She] 32; ---, she 31

2183. doubled. But]; ---, but 31+

2184. appeared:]; ---, 31+

2193-94. grace. She] 32; ---, she 31

2198. a<u>lone</u>,] 32; ---; 31

2199. <u>keeper</u>. <u>My</u>] 32; ---, <u>my</u> 31

2201. <u>inlargment</u>. <u>It</u>] 32; ---: <u>it</u> 31

2202. <u>time</u>;]; ---, 31

2204. <u>Consideration</u>. The] 32; ---; the 31

2212. <u>desire</u>. <u>If</u>]; ---, <u>if</u> 31

2216. <u>Lords</u>,] 32; Ls. 31

2218. <u>Prince</u>. She] 32; ---; she 31

2221. <u>Winchester</u>] 32; <u>Winch</u>. 31

2225. Queenes] 32; Q. 31

2226. her. <u>No</u>] 32; ---; <u>no</u> 31

2226. ne're]; <u>ner'e</u> 31

2227. <u>thought</u>;]; ---, 31

2228. good. Well] 32; ---; well 31

2230. Liberty.] 32; ---; 31

2234. selfe. Why] 32; ---; why 31

2236-37. imprisonment. What] 32; ---; what 31

2239. it;]; ---, 31+

2241. all.] 32; ---: 31

2241-42. departed. Seven] 32; ---ᴧ seven 31

2244. Roofe;]; ---, 31

2247. seene.] 32; ---; 31

2254. night. Whereupon] 32; ---, whereupon 31

2263. contrary. Whereunto] 32; ---; whereunto 31

2264. answered,] 32; ---; 31

2266. innocence;] 32; ---, 31

2267. out.] 32; ---; 31

2269. hands.] 32; ---; 31

2272. imprisoned.] 32; ---: 31

2273. you. Why] 32; ---, why 31

2274. others.] 32; ---; 31

2280. all.] 32; ---; 31

2286. hee,] H; ---ᴧ 31

2289. deliverance. She] 32; ---, she 31

2290. be;]; ---, 31

2294. mouth. Within] 32; ---, within 31

2295. after,] 32; ---ᴧ 31

2297. that] 32; ---, 31

2299. her. The] 32; ---, the 31

2300. happy;]; ---, 31

2305. mouth]; ---, 31+

2312. time,]; ---, 31

2312-13. which . . . said,] 32; (--- . . . ---) 31

2313-14. time. But] 32; ---; but 31

2314. Gardiner] 32; Gar. 31

2316. actions;]; ---, 31

2318. Winchester,] 32; ---, 31

2320. Elizabeth;]; ---, 31

2321. it. It] 32; ---, it 31

2325. The] 32; [No ¶] --- 31

2329. it] 41; ---, 31

2333. consumed. At] 32; ---, at 31

2335. thereof. He] 32; ---, he 31

2336. said,] 32; ---; 31

2337. dinner. The] 32; ---, the 31

2342. voyd] 32; ---, 31

2343. otherwise. Lying] 32; ---, lying 31

2348. now? Then] 32; ---, then 31

2349. it;] 32; ---, 31

2351. together. More] 32; ---: more 31

2358. appeare. She] 32; ---, she 31

2362. abroad] 32; ---, 31

2370. Heyre] 32; ---, 31

2374. <u>Regent</u>. But] 32; ---; but 31

2377. <u>Lachrymae</u>;] H; ---, 31

2379. poynt. It] 32; ---; it 31

2384. policy. But] 32; ---, but 31

2393. months. During] 32; ---, during 31

2396. it. How] 32; ---, how 31

2399. The] 32; the 31

2404. extremities. She] 32; ---, she 31

2408. lowest;]; ---, 31+

2410. designes. But] 32; ---, but 31

2413. apprehensions. Her] 32; ---, her 31

2422. Princesse.] 32; ---; 31

2423. natives (<u>It</u>] 32; ---; ˄--- 31

2423. &c);]; ---˄: 31

2430. Gaolers. But] 32; Goalers; but 31

2441-42. before. For] 32; ---; for 31

2455. here;] H; ---, 31

2456. brim. Perceiving] 32; ---, perceiving 31

2459. expired. They] 32; ---, they 31

2461. buried,] 32; ---˄ 31

2468. dunghill. Nay] 32; ---; nay 31

2470. free. Now] 32; ---, now 31

2475. them. Newes] 32; ---, newes 31

2475. over]; ---, 31+

2479. memorable.] 32; ---; 31

2482. dayes.] 32; ---; 31

2483. heart;] H; ---, 31

2488. land.] 32; ---; 31

2501. uncurable; then]; ---, then 31

2502. Parliament. Many]; ---, many 31+

2504. do;] H; ---, 31

2505. Queenes] 32; Qu. 31

2505. stomack. She] ; ---, she 31

2507. thereof,]; ---; 31+

2511. opened. Her] 32; ---; her 31

2518. 1558,] 32; ---. 31

2522. selfe;]; ---, 31

2526. vengeance. It] 32; ---, it 31

2536. winter.] 32; ---: 31

2536. Westminster,] 32; Westminst. 31

2543. Elizabeth] H; EliZabeth 31

2545. Hatfield] 32; ---, 31

2546. Charterhouse. From]; ---, from 31

2551. Elizabeth] H; Elizab. 31

2557. words:] 32; ---. 31

2566. Lyons:] 32; ---, 31

2567. delivered. To] 32; ---; to 31

2572. view. The] 32; ---, the 31

2573. thunder;]; ---, 31

2575. entertained] 32; ---, 31

2583-84. her. Amongst] 32; ---; amongst 31

2589. thankes.] 32; ---: 31

2600. Speaker,]; ---: 31

2603. One] 32; one 31

2605. hither. But] 32; ---; but 31

2606. Shee] 32; shee 31

2607. Truth,] H; ---, 31

2608. answered,]; ---; 31+

2610-11. over. Then] 32; ---; then 31

2615. stay. In] 32; ---; in 31

2621. is]; ---, 31+

2624. people. No] 32; ---; no 31

2625. power.] 32; ---; 31

2628. safely] 32; ---, 31

2631. behalfe.] 32; ---, 31

2633. Hospitall] 32; ---, 31

2634. governours. Shee] 32; ---, shee 31

2638. saying:]; ---; 31+

2638. all;] H; ---, 31

PRESS VARIANTS IN 1631

Of twenty extant copies, the following eight were
collated in full: F(1) (Folger Shakespeare Library), HD
(Harvard University Library), N (Newberry Library), TEX
(University of Texas), WIS (University of Wisconsin), BL(1)
(British Library 610.a.30), DUR (Durham University Library),
Bod. (Bodleian Library). The variants found in these copies
were checked in twelve other copies: F(2), F(3) (Folger Shake-
speare Library), LC (Library of Congress), CH (Chapin Library,
Williams College), STAN (Stanford University Library), Yale
(Beinecke Rare Book and Manuscript Library, Yale University),
HN (Henry E. Huntington Library), PML (Pierpont Morgan
Library), PENN (University of Pennsylvania), JRU (John
Rylands University Library of Manchester), BL (2) (British
Library 10805.aa.37), BL(3) (British Library G.1509).

Sheet A, inner forme

Corrected: F(1-3), N, CH, STAN, Yale, PML, BL(1), BL(3),
          DUR, JRU

Uncorrected: HD, TEX, WIS, LC, PENN, Bod.
    [Leaves A9–A12 lacking in HN; A12 lacking in BL(2).]

  Sig. A12r; ll. 98-99   H. H.] K. H.

Sheet D, outer forme

Corrected: F(3), N, TEX, WIS, CH, STAN, Yale, HN, PML, PENN,
          BL(1), BL(3), DUR, JRU

Uncorrected: F(1-2), HD, LC, Bod., BL(2)

  Sig. D2v; l. 675   conveniĕce] convenient [See Textual
      Notes.]

  Sig. D11r; page no.   69] 67

6. of the] In 31, "of the" ends a line and is then repeated at the beginning of the following line. Such repetition is a common error for Beale's compositor; see "Textual Introduction."

17. both cruell and] There would be little reason for the printer to add these words; they are almost certainly authorial.

24. he] The sense here is that, for all the help Hunsdon was to Elizabeth, it "makes me something to wonder . . . that he . . . should not bee so much as once remembred." Convoluted and obscure as Heywood's sentences occasionally become, he is unlikely to get both the gender and the case of a pronoun incorrect. It is much more likely that the compositor, having just set a number of lines dealing with Elizabeth, in which "her" is used six times (ll. 17-24) and "he" not at all, simply continued to see "her" and to set all three letters.

44. flee] The distinction in meaning between "flye" and "flee" is so slight in this context that one suspects compositorial misreading or foul case here. However, since the same change is made at l. 1989, and since the word is used in the same sense in both places (i.e., in the context of seeking shelter or safety), it can perhaps be taken to be an authorial emendation.

44-45. those words] This reading clarifies the sense of the paragraph as the "that" of 31 does not. In 31 the referent for "that" is "boldnesse"; the passage may therefore be paraphrased: "If my boldness offends you I will take comfort in the boldness of Claudian." The Latin quotation states that the lion kills those animals bold enough to wander from the herd; it is thus not an unqualified assertion of the worth of boldness. The 32 reading creates an appropriate sense of modesty and the passage may then be paraphrased: "If my boldness offends you, I must remember the words of Claudian--that

153

those who dare to be bold are also those who are, by their boldness, most easily destroyed."

135. enjoying] 31's "enjoyning" is an error similar to that of "blessngs" at l. 1955; in both cases, the "n" of "ing" was set before the "i." In the latter case, of course, the "i" was overlooked altogether. Although there are two OED definitions of "enjoin" which could perhaps be wrenched into making sense here ("To join together" and "To take part in"), the emended reading is clearly superior.

144. Prerogative] The word is generally used in the singular, even when it connotes more than one right or privilege, as in "the King's prerogative" (see citations in OED). The singular is also required here by the verb "was."

163. Henry] 31's reading "Edward" is curious here because of a sidenote which clearly states "Prince Henry borne." If the error had been caught before the forme went to the press it would have been relatively easy to correct the note because the name stands alone on a line; correcting the name in the text would have required changes in two lines because the word is hyphenated "Ed-|ward." This is not a wholly satisfactory explanation however; Henry requires only one less piece of type than Edward, and the resetting should not have been difficult.

238. In] "In," as a preposition, was "formerly (and still sometimes) used, where at, on, during, for are now in use . . . " (OED, def. 20). OED cites 2HenIV: "But look you pray . . . that our armies join not in a hot day" (I, ii, 207-08). 32 alters the reading to "On," but since it is unlikely that 31 is a misreading, and since Heywood often uses unusual and somewhat obsolete terms, I have chosen to retain the copy-text reading.

284. whose] The 31 reading "whsoe" is obviously incorrect and may have arisen from the compositor's selecting several pieces of type at the same time and then placing them in the stick in the wrong order. The same kind of problem appears with the misplaced apostrophes in "confin'd" (l. 894) and in "ne're" (l. 2226) and with "temperet" (l. 2454).

401. William] I find no reference to a Medlin Brierton, and all of Heywood's sources report the name correctly. "Medlin" is not an impossible misreading of MS "William."

532. languages] Although "language" can be used in the plural sense, Heywood is here naming specific languages and probably intended the plural. The plural also establishes a slight parallel with "Arts," and Heywood is often aware of such small niceties.

555. life of] The "of" was overlooked in 31; it is necessary for the sense.

660. as to be] The compositor probably read "to be" in "to be redressed" in the line above, without noticing the necessary "as" on the preceding line.

675. convenient speed she] When the compositor of 31 first set this passage, he ended a line with "convenient," then omitted the next two words—the object of the adjective, and the subject of the sentence—thus making gibberish of the passage: "That done, with all convenient returned backe into the Country. . . ." The omission was caught by the proofreader, but it was impossible to add the two words without resetting the remainder of the page and perhaps the following one also. Changing "convenient" to "conveniĕce" (see the list of press variants) involved no additional pieces of type and rendered the passage slightly clearer by eliminating the adjective.

680. Protector] As he often did, the compositor of 31 began the word at the end of a line, setting "Pro-," then set the whole word at the beginning of the next line. Since "Pro-" is also the last word on the page (sig. D2v), he may have thought he had set it as the catchword, though in fact he set "tector" as the catchword.

775-76. they . . . him] Although it would be correct to say that Edward was "borne with them" ("the liberall Arts"), the phrase "he appeared rather innate" is illogical. The use of "he" and "them" also does not make sense with the final clause of the sentence ("then . . . study"). Heywood's handwriting may have caused the misreading.

895. Durham] I find no record of a place named "Duresme," or of Durham having ever had the name. It probably arises from a compositorial misreading of the MS.

928. although] The occasional omission of a letter is not unusual for Beale's compositor; cf. 11. 323, 1955, 2025, 2417, 2561. The misreadings at 11. 532 ("languages"), 1170, 1511 ("Lord"), and 2333 ("quit") may arise from the same sort

of accidental omission. Words with "ough" seem especially prone to error (cf. ll. 952 and 1296).

983–84. a settled and unmooved] 31 reads "a settled & and unmooved," perhaps a compositorial error for "a settled & an unmooved," which improves the parallelism and eliminates the "a . . . unmooved" problem. It is just as likely, however, that the compositor read "and," set an ampersand, looked back at his copy and set "and." This second explanation is made even more plausible by the fact that "&" ends a line and "and" begins the next; Beale's compositor was particularly prone to duplication in this circumstance.

992. and] 31's "where being" garbles the sentence badly. The compositor may have read "where" for "there," though that is unlikely. Heywood probably just got lost in his syntax.

1170. removed] Although "remove" reads correctly in its own clause, it produces a rather abrupt shift in perspective when the reader encounters "brought" in the clause following.

1227. of her] The "f" does not print in any copies, and has apparently fallen out. There is space for it.

1451. your] The entire passage "Well . . . Grace" is something of a puzzle. 31, presumably following copy, sets direct discourse in italic. Here, however, the sentence "Well if it prove so . . . it will be the better for you" is in roman. 32, which quite often is not faithful to 31's italic, prints the sentence in italic. The indirect quotation "God blesse her Grace" should, by 31's conventions, have been in roman. My emendation from 32 assumes that Heywood intended the line to be italic, and therefore to be direct discourse, and therefore to read "your" instead of "her"; put another way: 31 is more likely to set the correct font than to set the correct words.

1511. Lords] Since there is more than one other nobleman present and no one in particular is singled out in the sentence, the sense would seem to require the plural.

1651. Crofts] There seems to have been some confusion about this name. Although Foxe always gives the name as "Croft," Holinshed uses both "Croft" (III, 907) and "Acroft" (IV, 126). This same disparity appears in Christopher Ockland's Elizabeth Queene: the name "Chroftes" is given in the text, but a sidenote reads "Syr Iames a Croftes" (sig.

D4r). Similarly, Camden (<u>Annales</u>) gives both "Crofts" (sig.
A4v) and "Croft" (sig. H2r). The 1632 reading might therefore
be considered a regularization rather than an actual correction, though the emender himself may have considered that he
was correcting an error.

1654. <u>Ashridge</u>] There is no place named "Abridge"; the
name is given correctly at l. 1168. But see "<u>Ashbridge</u>" in
<u>If</u> <u>You</u> <u>Know</u> <u>Not</u> <u>Me</u>, Part I, l. 113.

1761. by-] <u>OED</u> does not give the form "by-house," but
it is almost certainly what Heywood intended. It is formed,
presumably, on the analogy of "by-room," "a side or private
room." Cf. <u>1HenIV</u>, II, iv, 29-30.

1820. Gaoler] The compositor may simply have set the
"a" and "o" in the wrong order (see my note to l. 284), but
it is also quite possible that he misread his copy. Tannenbaum has pointed out that "Thomas Heywood's <u>a</u>'s and <u>o</u>'s are
often indistinguishable" (<u>Shakesperian</u> <u>Scraps</u> <u>and</u> <u>Other</u>
<u>Elizabethan</u> <u>Fragments</u> [New York: Columbia Univ. Press, 1933],
p. 120).

1932. <u>Bone-fires</u>] Although the hyphen occurs at the end
of a line I have retained it because in at least one other
place (where line-ending is no problem) Heywood hyphenates:
"that night were great Bone-fires made in the City and
Suburbs" (<u>The</u> <u>Life</u> <u>of</u> <u>Merlin</u>, sig. 2T2r).

1973. another] <u>OED</u> cites "a nother" as a legitimate
form, but in 31 the "a" appears at the end of a line, and
there is space after it for a hyphen which either fell out
or did not print.

1990. Cup] Heywood seldom has a subject disagree in
number with a verb, as 31's "Cups" does.

2169. faine to] Most <u>OED</u> definitions of "fain" are:
glad, willingly, eager. Definition A.2, however, is:
"Const. <u>to</u> with <u>inf</u>. Glad under the circumstances; glad or
content to take a certain course in default of opportunity
for anything better, or as the lesser of two evils." See
also definition A.2.b.: "This passes gradually into the
sense: Necessitated, obliged."

2286. perceiving] Since 31 does not have a comma
following "hee" in the preceding line, "perceived" makes
perfect sense until one reads "did forthwith take order."

Although I suspect that 31 omitted an ampersand between "trial" and "did," 32's reading also straightens out the grammar, and it has more authority than has mere conjecture.

2333. quite] 31's "quit" comes at the end of a rather crowded line (sig. K7r) and the "e" may have been dropped on purpose.

2343. Lying] In a number of copies of 31 the "g" has fallen out.

2344. Chichester] "Winchester" is obviously an error since Gardiner himself was Bishop of Winchester. George Day is the person referred to.

2360. God] It is inconceivable that Heywood, a good Protestant and ardent admirer of Elizabeth, intended her to pray to more than one god.

2461-62. the one . . . Michaels] It is possible that someone in the Cambridge printing house caught the error in 31 and cared enough to correct it, but it is more likely that Heywood, a former student at Cambridge, is responsible for the correction.

2515. these] The "there" of 31 may have resulted from foul case or from a misreading of copy. 32's omission of the word is a slight improvement but it requires "Her conceptions . . . unkindnesse" to act as a complicated compound subject for the sentence.

2515. other] The sense obviously requires that "other" modify "discontentments." 31's genitive noun "others" forces the reader to see another person's troubles causing Mary's final illness.

SIDENOTES

The following list of sidenotes reproduces the readings
as they appear in the 1631 edition; u/v, i/j, and long "s"
have been modernized and tildes have been expanded, but other
contractions and abbreviations have been retained. Variant
substantive readings from the second and third editions are
in brackets; if there is no siglum, the variant is the same
in both the 1632 and 1641 editions. Each note is keyed to the
line number in the present edition at which the sidenote begins, but the original lineation of the notes themselves has
not been preserved. The notes occasionally do not begin at
exactly the same point in 32 and 41 as they do in 31, but the
difference is slight and no record is made of it except for
the notes at lines 2108 and 2113 which are reversed (and
thereby corrected) in 32 and 41.

115. Prince <u>Arthur</u> marrieth Infant <u>Katharine</u> of Spaine.

129. Prince <u>Henry</u> marrieth his Brothers wife.

138. The [mo?]tives perswading a Divorce.

162. Prince <u>Henry</u> borne.

174. The Divo-|vorce disputed of. [divorce]

192. Cardinall <u>Campeius</u> sent from Rome.

204. The Lady <u>Anne Bullein</u> daughter to the Earle of
     <u>Wiltshire</u> & <u>Ormond</u> created Marchionesse of
     <u>Pembrooke</u>.

228. <u>Henry</u> the eight married to the Lady <u>Anne Bullein</u>.

238. Queene <u>Anne</u> crowned.

251. The birth of the Lady <u>Elizabeth</u>.

253. Not kept a fortnight or a month in state, as it is
      now usuall with ordinary people.

256. Lady Elizabeth borne on the Eve of the virgins
      Nativity, and died on the Eve of the Virgins
      Annuntiation 1603 Even that she is now in heaven
      with all these blessed virgins that had oyle in
      their lampes. [1603. She is now . . . those
      blessed. . . .]

264. Lady Elizabeths godfather and godmothers.

268. An oath taken to the successors of Q. Anne.

276. The Reason of Qu. Annes so sudden coronation.

291. The different dispositions of Elizabeth and Mary.

304. The preparation to Queene Annes fall.

320. The Qu. Brothers with other sent to the Tower.
      [brother . . . others]

349. Queene Anne commanded to the tower.

363. Qu. Anne entreth the towuer

376. Qu. Anne arraigned.

389. Q. Anne quit in the opinion of the Lords, but found
      guilty by the Jury.

399. The Queens Brother with others beheaded.

408. Queene Annes death.

412. Her Speech at her death.

456. The Birth of P[r]ince Edward.

469. The death of Qu. Jane in Child-bed.

474. Young Edward Prince of Wales, &c [41: Young Edward
      created Prince. . . .]

483. Dr. Coxe and Sr John Cheeke Tutors to P. Edward and
      L. Elizabeth.

514. The Industry of the Prince and L. Eliz.

554. The Prince & La. Elizabeth not ingratefull to their
     Tutors.

572. The last Will and Testament of K. Henry the eighth.

592. K. Henry dyeth.

600. K. Henry buried at Windsor.

602. Edward the 6. crowned.

616. L. Elizabeths observance to the King her brother.

626. L. Elizabeth goeth into the countrey.

646. A Princely Husband offered to the L. Elizabeth.

652. L. Elizabeth will not by any meanes marry.

679. The Kings 3. Uncles.

686. Northumberland and Suffolke worke a division betwixt
     the two Brothers.

718. The L. Admiral beheaded.

723. The Protector questioned.

728. The Protector quit of treason.

734. The Protector found guilty of Felonie, & beheaded.

748. A Match betwixt Northumberlands Son and Suffo[l]k
     Daughter. [Suffolks]

751. The King dyeth.

754. La. Jane proclaymed Qu.

772. A true Character of K. Edward the 6.

801. He that shal but peruse the History of S George now
     written by M. Heylin, may soone goe beyond the L.
     Treasurers answer to the King.

820. The Kings Prayer at his death.

837. L. <u>Mary</u> vexed at the Proclamation of Q. <u>Jane</u>.

841. <u>Suffolke</u> men ayde the Lady <u>Mary</u>.

845. <u>Northumberland</u> opposeth the L. <u>Mary</u>.

857. Lady <u>Mary</u> proclaimed Queene.

878. L. <u>Elizabeth</u> lamenteth her Brothers death.

887. The L. <u>Eliz</u>. in policy graced by the Queene.

890. Protestant Bishops put off, Popish restored.

915. Q <u>Mary</u> crowned.

921. <u>Guilford</u> <u>Dudley</u> and L. <u>Jane</u> convicted of treason.

965. The Q. pittieth the Lady Jane.

973. No Protestant thought fit to live.

994. The La. <u>Jane</u> her speech at her death.

1036. Lady <u>Janes</u> death.

1039. A memorable note of Judge <u>Morgan</u>.

1045. Lady <u>Jane</u> thought to be with child at her death.

1049. A true Character of the L. <u>Jane</u>.

1085. The L. <u>Janes</u> Workes.

1093. <u>Suffolke</u> betrayed by his Servant.

1108. The Duke of <u>Suffolke</u> beheaded.

1115. The beginning of Qu. <u>Elizabeths</u> Troubles.

1149. <u>Gardiner</u> a bitter enemy to the L. <u>Elizabeth</u>.

1168. The Lady <u>Elizabeth</u> sent for out of the Countrey.

1173. Lo. of <u>Tame</u>, Sir <u>Edward</u> <u>Hastings</u>, Sir <u>Thomas</u>
      <u>Cornewallis</u> sent for the La. <u>Elizabeth</u>.

1179. L. <u>Eliz</u>. very sicke.

1202. Uncivill intrusion.

1215. La. Elizabeths loyalty.

1248. L. Elizabeth removeth towards London.

1254. The Peoples love to the L. Elizabeth.

1269. L. Elizabeth kept close at Court.

1278. [Virgil. Aen. 5.] [This note is not in 31.]

1292. La. Elizabeth brought before the Councell.

1304. La. Elizabeth answereth all objections.

1328. The La. Eliz. left alone at the Councel-board.

1338. La. Elizabeth commanded to the Tower.

1345. La. Elizabeth affraid of the Tower.

1348. La. Elizabeth her Speech to the Councell. [Her speech to. . . .]

1363. The Earle of Sussex a fast friend to the L. Eliz.

1390. La. Elizabeth commanded to the Tower.

1399. Earle of Sussex continues a fast friend to the L. Eliz. [The Earl. . . .]

1405. La. Elizabeth writeth to the Queene.

1423. La. Elizabeths speech at her departure out of the Court.

1432. La. Elizabeths danger in shooting London-Bridge.

1437. L. Eliz. landed at the Traitors staires. [41: om.]

1444. La Elizabeths speech at her landing in the Tower. [Her speech. . . .]

1454. La. Elizabeth delivered up to the Constable of the Tower. [The Lady. . . .]

1460. The inhumanity of the Constable towards the L. Elizabeth. [towards her.]

1465. The Earle of Sussex love to the L. Eliz.

1466. The Lieftenants courtesie to the La. Eliz. [courtesie to her.]

1477. La. Elizabeth lockt up close in the Tower.

1483. The La. Eliz. speech being lockt in her Chamber.

1503. The Lords take advice about a watch to keepe the L. Eliz. safe.

1506. The good E. of Sussex still a friend to the L. Eliz. [friend to her.]

1515. Masse said & sung in the La. Elizabeths Chamber.

1539. Phil. of Spaine landeth.

1545. The devotion of K. Phil.

1557. Philip commeth to Winchester.

1576. Phil. brought into the presence privately. [K. Philip]

1587. The courteous behaviour of Philip to the people. [K. Philip]

1589. Q. Maryes entertainment to Philip.

1610. The Marriage solemnized between Philip and Q. Mary.

1622. Philip and Q. Mary proclaimed King & Qu. of England, &c.

1632. Philip and Q. Mary dine together at one Table.

1637. Philip and Q. Mary passe through London in State.

1648. Gardiner examineth the L. Eliz. in the Tower.

1657. La. Elizabeths answer to the objections of Gardiner.

1673. Arondels kind reply to the L. Eliz.

1687. The severity of the Constable of the <u>Tower</u> to the
L. <u>Elizabeth</u>.

1702. Lo. <u>Shandois</u> moveth the Lords of the Councell on the
behalfe of the <u>L</u>. <u>Eliz</u>. [32: <u>on the behalf the</u>]

1705. La. <u>Elizabeth</u> suffered to have a Cazement open in her
Chamber.

1708. A Warrant for the Lady <u>Elizabeths</u> death. [41: <u>for
her death</u>.]

1709. Mr. <u>Bridges</u> made a happy instrument to preserve the
L. <u>Elizabeth</u>. [32: <u>an happy</u> . . . <u>to preserve her</u>.]

1721. The Constable of the Tower discharged, Sir <u>Henry
Benningfield</u> put in trust with the La. <u>Elizabeth</u>.

1727. La. <u>Elizabeth</u> removed to <u>Woostocke</u>. [<u>Woodstock</u>]

1734. La. <u>Elizabeth</u> afraid of Sir <u>Henry Benningfield</u>.

1759. La. <u>Elizabeth</u> feareth to be murthered at <u>Richmond</u>.
[<u>murdered</u>]

1766. La. <u>Elizabeth</u> receiveth comfort from her Gentleman
Usher.

1776. <u>La</u>. <u>Elizabeths</u> meditations.

1792. The noble resolution of the <u>Lord</u> of <u>Tame</u>.

1798. The Countreyes love to the <u>L</u>. <u>Eliz</u> in her passage to
<u>Woodstocke</u>.

1820. La. <u>Elizabeth</u> calleth Sir <u>Hen</u>: <u>Benningfield</u> her
<u>Gaoler</u>.

1834. <u>Tanquam ovis</u>, As a sheep to the slaughter.

1839. L. <u>Elizabeth</u> lodgeth at the <u>Lord</u> of <u>Tames</u> house.

1854. The saucy rude behaviour of Sir <u>Hen</u>. <u>Benning</u>.

1872. L. <u>Eliz</u>. lockt and bolted up in <u>Woodstocke</u> [<u>The
Lady</u>. . . .]

1877. The Keeper of <u>Woodstocke</u> attempted to kill the <u>La</u>.
<u>Elizabeth</u>. [<u>kill her</u>.]

1887. <u>La</u>. <u>Elizabeths</u> liberty to walke in the Gardens.

1897. <u>La</u>. <u>Elizabeths</u> meditatious as she walked in the
Garden. [<u>meditations</u>]

1929. <u>La</u>. <u>Elizabeth</u> almost burned in her bed.

1953. <u>La</u>. <u>Elizabeth</u> <u>thankfull</u> to God for her delivery out
of the fire.

1958. <u>La</u>. <u>Elizabeths</u> prayer in the midst of her sorrow.
[41 sets the note as a heading in the text.]

2004. <u>La</u>. <u>Elizabeth</u> desireth to write to the Queene.

2013. <u>S</u>. <u>Henry</u> <u>Benningfield</u> will not suffer any one but
himselfe to convey the <u>La</u>. <u>Elizabeths</u> Letter to the
Qu. [41: <u>letters</u>]

2040. Sir <u>Hen</u>. <u>Benningfield</u> keepeth L. <u>Eliz</u>. Letters foure
dayes after they were dated.

2048. <u>La</u>. <u>Elizabeth</u> sicke.

2049. The Qu. sendeth two physitians to the La. <u>Elizabeth</u>.

2053. The Physitians returne a good report of the L. <u>Eliz</u>.
to the Qu.

2062. Divers tamper with the L. <u>Elizabeth</u> to have her to
submit her selfe to the Queene.

2067. <u>La</u>. <u>Elizabeths</u> answer concerning her submission.

2081. Sir <u>Hen</u>: <u>Benningfield</u> sent for to the Councell-
board.

2082. Consultation what to doe with the La. <u>Elizabeth</u>.
[<u>Consultations</u>]

2087. One of the Lords and <u>Gardiners</u> sodaine advice.

2095. The <u>Spaniards</u> love to the L. <u>Elizabeth</u>.

2108. A great danger escaped. [At line 2117 in 32, 41.]

2113. A great conspiracie against the L. Elizabeth.
     [At line 2105 in 32, 41.]

2128. La. Elizabeth wisheth her selfe a Milke-maide. [om.]

2133. Queen Mary bruited to bee with Child.

2138. K. Philip favoureth the La. Elizabeth.

2150. La. Elizabeths farewell written in the glass window
     at Woodstocke. [41: Elisabeth]

2156. The La. Eliz. commanded up to Court. [She is
     commanded. . . .]

2167. Sir Hen Benningfield cruelty to the L. Eliz.
     [Benningfields]

2184. The L. Wil. Howard comforteth the La. Eliz.

2191. Gardiner, Arondell, Shrewsbury, Peter present
     themselves lovingly to the Lady Elizabeth.

2195. L. Elizabeth. speech to the Lords [Her speech. . . .]

2204. Gardiners answer to the L. Elizabeth [to her.]

2208. L. Elizabeths resolute answer to Gardiner.

2221. Gardiner with other Lords repaire to her lodging the
     next day. [41: Lord]

2241. La Elizabeth lock'd up seven days in Court before she
     spake with the Qu. [in the Court]

2247. K. Philips friendship to the L. Elizabeth.

2251. L. Elizabeth commeth before the Qu.

2260. L. Elizabeth protesteth loyalty to the Queene,
     [She protesteth her loyalty. . . .]

2263. The Queene sharpely answereth the L. Elizabeth.

2300. L. Elizabeth committed to her loving friends.
     [The Lady. . . .]

2304. Gardiners pursuit in mischeife.

2310. Foure Gentl-|women of the L. Elizabeth committed to prison at once. [32: Elisabeths]

2320. Fox. acts and Monuments.

2331. A just judgement upon Gardiner.

2352. Gardiner had enflamed many Martyrs, and hath now his body enflamed.

2355. Divers of the Ladies, Adversarie drop away. [adversaries]

2368. Reports spred abroad that Queene Mary was delivered of a Sonne, but afterwards proved false.

2386. K. Philip resolveth for the low-Countreis.

2392. K. Philips stay, the Papists opportunity.

2422. L. Elizabeth troubles compared with those of her raigne. [Elisabeths]

2436. The malice of Cardinall Poole, Bonner, anothers. [and others.]

2441. 2[6?]0 put to death in Qu. Maries raigne

2455. The bones of Martin Bucer and Paulus Phagius burnt

2482. The cause of Qu Maries death

2518. On a Thursday died King Henry the eight and Ed. the sixth, Qu. Mary &c. [32, 41 omit and; 41: One a Thursday. . . .]

2522. Non natura sed Pontificiorum arte ferox.

2525. Men of blood shall not live halfe their dayes. Psal. 55. [live out half . . . Psal.55.23]

2540. La. Elizabeth proclaimed Queene of England.

2550. Q. Elizabeth passeth thorow London.

2558. Q. Elizabeths prayer comming out of the Tower. [41 sets this as a subheading.]

2595.   Qu. <u>Elizabeths</u> answer to the Speaker.

2608.   Qu. <u>Elizabeth</u> receiveth the Bible lovingly.

2620.   Q. <u>Elizabeths</u> speech to the City.

2621.   Q. <u>Elizabeths</u> grand-fathers fathers [sic] was a Lord
         Maior of London.   [41: <u>Elisabeth</u>; 32, 41: <u>father</u>]

2632.   Q. <u>Elizabeth</u> pleased with the sight of the Children
         of Christs Hospitall.

HYPHENATED LINE ENDINGS

The reading to the left of the bracket is from the present edition; that to the right is the form in 1631.

   2.   <u>Viscount</u>] <u>Vis-</u>|<u>count</u>

  12.   Kinsman] Kins-|man

 177.   upwards] up-|wards

 308.   Bedchamber] Bed-|chamber

 518.   Breakfast-time] Breakfast-|time

 821.   <u>howbeit</u>] <u>how-</u>|<u>beit</u>

 874.   indifferent] in-|different

 934.   <u>albeit</u>] <u>al-</u>|<u>beit</u>

1004.   therewithall] there-|withall

1025.   Gentlewomen] Gentle-|women

1129.   Holy-dayes] Holy-|dayes

1177.   horsemen] horse-|men

1204.   bed-side] bed-|side

1217.   withall] with-|all

1258.   safeguard] safe-|guard

1333.   Sun-shine] Sun-|shine

1411.   midnight] mid-|night

1551.   <u>Watergate</u>] <u>Water-</u>|<u>gate</u>

1562. Singingmen] Singing-|men

1596. torch-light] torch-|light

1625. Arch-Dukes] Arch-|Dukes

1757. <u>Wood-stocke</u>] <u>Wood-|stocke</u>

1884. Tenterhooks] Tenter-|hooks

1900. grashopper] gras-|hopper

1905. Sun-beame] Sun-|beame

1932. <u>Bone-fires</u>] <u>Bone-|fires</u>

2148. <u>Smithweeke</u>] <u>Smith-|weeke</u>

2195. re-saluted] re-|saluted

2444. Husbandmen] Husband-|men

2474. handwriting] hand-|writing

EXPLANATORY NOTES

(Biographical information, including direct quotation, is
from the Dictionary of National Biography, unless otherwise
noted.)

1. Lord HENRY] Elder son of John Carey, third Lord
Hunsdon (d. 1617) and Mary Hyde. Heywood also dedicated
Pleasant Dialogues and Dramas (STC 13358; 1637) to him.

10. Henry Lord Hunsdon] Henry Carey (1524?-1596), first
Baron Hunsdon, was a cousin of Elizabeth and Lord Chamberlain
of her household. He served on the commission which tried
Mary Queen of Scots (DNB), and occasionally acted as licenser
for the press (see W. W. Greg, Licensers for the Press, &c.
to 1640 [Oxford: Oxford Bibliographical Society, 1962]).

55-56. Leones . . . relinquunt.] "Lions soon leave
destroyed those things that are bold enough to stray."
Claudian's Deprecatio ad Hadrianum (11. 28-29) reads
"leones, quae stravisse calent, eadem prostrata relinquunt."

66. Polypragmatist] "a busybody" (OED)

67. Sed meliora spero.] "But I hope for better things."

80. sappy] "full of vitality"; "full of 'goodness' or
substance"; "immature, unseasoned." For this last definition
OED cites John Hayward's The life and raigne of King Edward
the Sixt (STC 12998; 1630): "When he had passed this weake
and sappie age, he was committed to Dr. Coxe" (sig. A2r).

97. vix ea nostra voco] "I can scarcely call these
things my own."

98-99. H. H.] Henry Holland (1583-1650?), son of the
translator Philemon Holland and brother of the poet Abraham
Holland, was a bookseller in London from 1609 to 1647. His
two most important compilations were Baziliωlogia, a book of
kings, beeing . . . effigies of all our English Kings

(STC 13581; 1618) a collection of thirty-one engraved portraits, and Herwologia Anglica (STC 13582; 1620) containing
sixty-five portraits of important persons from Henry VIII
through the reign of Elizabeth. (See R. B. McKerrow et al.,
A Dictionary of Printers and Booksellers . . . 1557-1640
[Oxford: The Bibliographical Society, 1910], pp. 140-41; for
a detailed analysis of both works, see Hind, Engraving in
England in the Sixteenth & Seventeenth Centuries, II,
115-39, 145-62.) Heywood wrote commendatory verses to both
father and son in Philemon Holland's translation of
Xenophon's Cyrupaedia (STC 26068; 1632; sigs. ¶¶ 2r-v).

107. N. R.] These initials have not been identified.
Collier saw them, and Heywood's reference to "my Poeme" (1.
70), as evidence that the preface "must . . . have belonged
to some other production upon the same subject, and that
production a poem" (J. Payne Collier, ed., Two Historical
Plays on the Life and Reign of Queen Elizabeth [i.e., I and
II If You Know Not Me], Shakespeare Society Publications no.
45 [London: Shakespeare Society, 1851], p. x). Collier is
probably taking Heywood's use of "Poeme" too literally. In
a commendatory poem prefacing Heywood's Philocothonista,
George Donne (the son of the poet) addresses him as
"Nephaliophilus," and on the basis of this reference Bates
asserts that "N. R." "may refer to some nickname known to
his circle" (Katharine Lee Bates, ed., A Woman Killed With
Kindness and The Fair Maid of the West, Belles-Lettres
Series [Boston: Heath, 1917], p. lxv). Bates also raises
the point about "my Poeme" but has no reservations about
assigning Englands Elizabeth to Heywood.

166. Saint Mathews day] The actual date of death (22
February) is closer to St. Mathias day (24 February) than to
St. Mathews (21 September). The error may have arisen from a
compositorial misreading of the MS, but Heywood made the same
mistake ten years later (perhaps because he was borrowing from
Englands Elizabeth) when, in The Life of Merlin (Wing H1786;
1641), he wrote that "prince Henry the Kings sonne . . . died
upon S. Matthews day the yeere following" (sig. 2S1r). A more
likely origin for the error is to be found in Heywood's
sources, who report the death as occurring on "the euen of
sainct Mathy" (Hall's Chronicle, ed. Henry Ellis [1809; rpt.
New York: AMS, 1965], p. 519) or "the euen of saint Matthie"
(Holinshed, III, 561).

232. Rowland Lee] (d. 1543). Bishop of Coventry and
Lichfield. Early in his career he worked actively with Wolsey
in the suppression of the monasteries. He was in Henry's ser-

vice from 1531 to 1534. "It has often been asserted that the
crowning service by which Lee earned his bishopric was the
celebration of the secret marriage between Henry and Anne
Boleyn." Some reports (mostly Catholic) suggest that Henry
tricked Lee into performing the marriage by telling him that
he had a license from the Pope. In mid-1534 he was appointed
president of the Kings Council in the marches of Wales, where
most of the remainder of his life was spent in "the rooting
out of Welsh disorder" (DNB). According to A. F. Pollard,
"the See of Coventry and Lichfield was often called Chester
before the creation of the latter see" (Henry VIII [1902; rpt.
New York: Harper, 1966], p. 254, n. 2).

234-37. Anne Savage . . . Berkely] Anne Savage was the
daughter of Sir John Savage of Frodsham, Chestershire, and the
second wife (after Mary Hastings, daughter of the first Earl
of Huntingdon, died) of Thomas Lord Berkeley (1505-1534), who
was called to Parliament in 1533. (Peter Townend, ed.,
Burke's Genealogical and Heraldic History of the Peerage . . .,
105th ed. [London: Burke's Peerage Ltd., 1970], p. 246.)

262. Dutchesse of Norfolke] Wife of Thomas Howard,
Earl of Surrey and second Duke of Norfolk.

266. Marchionesse of Dorset] Widow of Thomas Grey,
second Marquis of Dorset. He was one of the witnesses
against Queen Catherine.

268. oath of allegiance] STC 7780, An acte declarynge
the establysshment of the succession (15 January 1534).
"The words of the oath were not included in the act, but
they were formulated on the last day of the session and the
oath was taked by members of parliament, ministers, and
others before it was given statutory sanction in a second
act of succession which was passed when parliament
reassembled in November" (J. D. Mackie, The Earlier Tudors
1485-1558 [Oxford: Clarendon Press, 1952], p. 359).

307. Henry Norrice] Courtier and at one time a
favorite of Henry. "Henry is said . . . to have offered
Norris a pardon if he would admit his crime" (Pollard, p.
276).

337. Thomas Audley] (1488-1544). Lord Chancellor and
Speaker of the House of Commons.

337-38. Thomas Cromwell] Earl of Essex (1485?-1540).
He held numerous high positions under Henry: Chancellor of

the Exchequer, King's Secretary, Vicar-general, Lord Great
Chamberlain of England. He encouraged and arranged Henry's
marriage to Anne of Cleves but fell quickly and somewhat mys-
teriously from grace after being accused of treason by the
Duke of Norfolk. He was beheaded on the day Henry married
Norfolk's niece Catherine Howard; she was given the lands
Cromwell had been awarded for his part in the dissolution of
the monasteries. (<u>DNB</u>; J. J. Scarisbrick, <u>Henry VIII</u>
[Berkeley and Los Angeles: Univ. of California Press, 1968],
pp. 429-30.)

339. <u>William Kinsman</u>] William Kingston (d. 1540) became
Constable of the Tower in 1524; in 1539 he was made Controller
of the King's Household and a Knight of the Garter.

376-77. Duke of <u>Norfolk</u>] Thomas Howard (1473-1554),
Earl of Surrey and third Duke of Norfolk. Anne was his
niece; her mother, Elizabeth Howard, was Thomas's sister.

384. accusations] The major charges were adultery,
incest, and (therefore) treason. Most scholars believe the
charges were trumped-up: "Certainly she had been indiscreet
with Mark Smeaton, . . . with Norris and perhaps one Francis
Weston, seeing too much of them, dancing too familiarly with
them, sharing too many romantic secrets with them. But it
is difficult to believe that she was ever guilty of adultery
with them, or of incest with her brother" (Scarisbrick, pp.
349-50). However, Pollard, attempting to counter the popular
off-with-her-head picture of Henry, points out that "if the
charges were merely invented to ruin the Queen, one culprit
besides herself would have been enough. To assume that Henry
sent four needless victims to the block is to accuse him of a
lust for superfluous butchery, of which even he, in his most
bloodthirsty moments, was not capable" (p. 277). E. W. Ives
sees the trial and execution of both Anne and the courtiers as
a consequence of factions within the court, with the guilt or
innocence of the victims having little real bearing on the
matter ("Faction at the Court of Henry VIII: the Fall of Anne
Boleyn," <u>History</u>, 57 [1972], 169-88).

387. Auditory] "audience." From the context here, it
seems not to be meant in the sense of "jury." Heywood uses
the word in a similar sense in the preface to <u>Gunaikeion</u>,
where he explains that he has included some jesting tales in
his collection, "least the Auditorie should be dulled with
serious courses" (sig. A4v).

400. <u>Marke Smeton</u>] A court musician, the only one of

those accused of adultery with the Queen to confess (under threat of torture).

401. William Brierton] Usually spelled Brereton. Little is known of him; Wriothesley says that he was a gentleman of the Privy Chamber and that he and Smeaton were buried in the same grave in a churchyard within the Tower (Charles Wriothesley, A Chronicle of England During the Reigns of the Tudors, ed. William Douglas Hamilton, Camden Society [1875; rpt. New York: Johnson, 1965], I, 36, note h, 40). He was from Shocklach, and married Elizabeth Somerset, daughter of the first Earl of Worcester (DNB, Supp., p. 264).

401. Francis Weston] (1511?-1536); a Gentleman of the Privy Chamber and former page to Henry.

435-38. Phoenix . . . duos.] "Here lies the Phoenix, Anne, born to be a Phoenix, sorrowfully. Generations of Phoenixes have not produced two (i.e., another like her)."

484. Doctor Coxe] Richard Cox (1500-1581) served as Edward's tutor from July 1544 until early in 1550. In exile during Mary's reign, he returned to England in 1559 and was made Bishop of Ely.

484-85. John Cheeke] Cheke (1514-1557), "unquestionably one of the most learned men of his age," had been a student of George Day's at St. John's College, Cambridge. Under Edward he became Secretary of State. Mary sent him to the Tower for his support of Lady Jane Grey; he fled to the continent but in 1556 was returned to the Tower, where, to save his life, he recanted.

486-87. Instructors . . . Lady] Cheke and Cox were Edward's tutors but seem to have had little to do with Elizabeth, who was tutored by William Grindall, one of Ascham's students, until his death early in 1548, at which time Ascham himself assumed the post and held it for about two years. See J. E. Neale, Queen Elizabeth I: A Biography (1934; rpt. Garden City, N. Y.: Doubleday, 1957), pp. 13-14.

509. horae matutinae] "morning hours"

532-36. Most . . . English] On Edward's attainments, linguistic and otherwise, see W. K. Jordan, Edward VI: The Young King (Cambridge, Mass.: Harvard Univ. Press, 1968), pp. 40-45. Elizabeth's facility with languages became a

commonplace in any description of her. Henry Chettle, e.g.,
wrote that she was "So expert in Languages that she answered
most Embassadors in their natiue tongues" (Englandes
Mourning Garment [STC 5121; 1603], sig. C3v). In a letter
of 4 April 1550, Ascham wrote of her: "She talks French and
Italian as well as English: she has often talked to me
readily and well in Latin, and moderately so in Greek" (J. A.
Giles, ed., The Whole Works of Roger Ascham [1865; rpt. New
York: AMS, 1965], I, pt. 1, lxiii; the original letter, in
Latin, is printed on pp. 181-93).

537-40. Merito . . . Pallas.] "As an extraordinary
child of the world, rightly she might be called Phoenix:
another virgin Pallas." Pallas (Athena, Minerva) was the
virgin goddess of defensive warfare, arts, wisdom, and
reason.

559. learned Sermon] "According to the Mantuan agent
in London . . . Cox inveighed against the monks as the
impious authors of the Marian persecution, and praised the
Queen whose divine mission it was to end such iniquities,
destroy the monasteries and all images, and purify the
Church. The sermon . . . lasted an hour and a half" (J. E.
Neale, Elizabeth I and Her Parliaments: 1559-1581 [New York:
St. Martin's Press, 1958], p. 42).

566. last will and Testament] The original is now in
the Public Record Office (Royal Wills, E.23, IV, pt. i, pp.
1-17). It is reprinted in Thomas Rymer's Foedera,
Conventiones, Literae . . . VI, pt. 3, 3rd ed. (1745; rpt.
Farnborough, England: Gregg Press, 1967), VI, 142-45.

627. Country] Chelsea, where she was to complete her
education under the tutelage of Katharine Parr. See Alison
Plowden, The Young Elizabeth (Newton Abbot: Readers Union,
1972), p. 83.

643. Governesse] Katherine Champernowne, Mistress Ashley, "a Devonshire woman of good education and good, though
impoverished, family." She was appointed a waiting gentle-
woman to Elizabeth in June 1536 by Thomas Cromwell; in 1545
she married John Ashley (or Astley), a cousin of Anne Boleyn
(Plowden, p. 67). Neale characterizes her as "a well-meaning,
affectionate, but not very sensible woman" (Queen Elizabeth,
p. 20). Called "Kat" by Elizabeth, she was a close friend and
confidante, and was imprisoned several times during Mary's
attempts to quash Elizabeth. At Elizabeth's accession she was
made chief Lady of the Bedchamber and her husband was appoint-

ed Keeper of the Jewel House (Plowden, p. 210). She died in
June 1565 (Elizabeth Jenkins, Elizabeth the Great [New York:
Coward, 1959], p. 115).

644-70. Scarce was she . . . retyred.] The facts here
are vague and the story may be apocryphal. The language
("Princely" and "retyred into his Countrey") suggests that
the "Suitor" was foreign, but there is no evidence that any
foreign marriage arrangements were being contemplated this
early. In the summer of 1547, Thomas Seymour (Lord High Admiral and one of Elizabeth's uncles via Jane Seymour) was
living in Chelsea with Elizabeth and his new bride Katharine
Parr; the infamous quasi-sexual play between the two--which
was later to embarrass Elizabeth and contribute to Seymour's
conviction for treason--can hardly be considered a courtship,
although after Katharine's death Seymour indicated, through
her steward Thomas Parry, that he would marry her (Neale,
Queen Elizabeth, pp. 17-18; Plowden, pp. 83-89, 97ff). A
similar version of Heywood's story is told by Christopher Ockland, in Elizabeth Queene (in The Valiant Acts of the English
Nation [STC 18777; 1585], sigs. C2v-C3r):

Of twise seuen yeares, the tender age she scarse had
                                        fully tract,
When that mature, the virgin might, for spousall rites
                                        exact,
When as behold, with portlike trayne, one unkle to the
                                        king,
Himselfe unto her Princely house, in pompous sort did
                                        bring,
And doth the tender Lady bright, with much ambition woe,
Forthwith through shame, with blushing hewe, her eares
                                did burning gloe[,]
Attending not what Hymen ment, nor what this wooing
                                        Peere,
With earnest sute did pray. Wherefore he parteth
                                nothing neere.
But he insistes againe and urgeth more his sute to winne,
Till from the princely Nimphe, he had that finall
                                answeare gin,
Declared by her governesse, he labour lost in vayne.

It is interesting that Heywood's explanation of this event as
determining Elizabeth's refusal to marry later (11. 668-70)
is echoed by a modern scholar writing about the Seymour
affair: "very possibly her later wariness in emotional in-
volvements stems from this unpleasant experience of her girlhood" (Jordan, The Young King, pp. 372-73).

687. <u>Gray</u>] Henry Grey (1517?-1554), Duke of Suffolk
and third Marquis of Dorset, father of Lady Jane Grey, was
present at Elizabeth's christening. He was convinced by
Northumberland to let his daughter marry Northumberland's
son and then to be declared queen on Edward's death. When
the council proclaimed Mary, Suffolk denied Jane and joined
in the proclamation. He opposed the marriage of Philip and
Mary, joined Wyat's rebellion, was captured in Warwickshire
(see Heywood's account at 11. 1090-1109), and was executed on
Tower Hill 23 February 1554 (<u>DNB</u>). Grey's combination of un-
realistic ambition, poor judgment, and weakness of character
made his fate virtually inevitable: "Grey managed to lend his
support to every frail and hopeless cause that presented itself throughout his short life" (Jordan, <u>The Young King</u>,
p. 92).

755-56. where hee was buryed] That Heywood saw some
question about this suggests that he was relying solely on
Foxe at this point, for, although Foxe recounts the St.
George story and prints Edward's final prayer (VI, 351-52),
he says nothing about the burial. The funeral was not kept
secret, but it did not attract the widespread attention
usual for such a state event: it was delayed until 8 August,
more than a month after the death; the ceremony was small,
with few English and no foreign dignitaries in attendance;
and no formal marker was erected (W. K. Jordan, <u>Edward VI:
The Threshold of Power</u> [Cambridge, Mass.: Harvard Univ.
Press, 1970], p. 520, n. 1). Nevertheless, Heywood's
declared source is in no doubt about the site: "jacet juxta
caput Avi sui Regis Henrici septimi in ejus Sacrario
Westmonasteriensi sub Altari ex aere deaurato & artificiose
elaborato" (Holland, <u>Herwologia</u>, sig. C1v). The site of the
burial is also mentioned in a number of other sources which
could have been available to Heywood, including Holinshed
(IV, 3), John Hayward (<u>The life and raigne</u>, sig. Z2r), and
William Baldwin (<u>The Funeralles of King Edward the sixt</u> [STC
1243; 1560], sig. C3v). Machyn, as might be expected, gives
a detailed description of the funeral procession; though he
never mentions the exact burial site, he does say that there
was a "hersse in Westmynster abbay" (Henry Machyn, <u>The Diary
of Henry Machyn</u>, ed. John Gough Nichols, Camden Society
[1848; rpt. New York: AMS, 1968], pp. 39-40).

778. <u>ad unguem</u>] "precisely; to perfection"

779. <u>punctilio</u>] "minute detail"

786. Inchoation] "beginning"

786. Instauration] OED cites this passage from Englands
Elizabeth under the definition "institution, founding, estab-
lishment."

788. Cardanus] Hieronymus Cardano, an Italian
physician and astrologer. Cardano met Edward in 1552 and
cast his horoscope; his observations on the king's learning
were published in Geniturarum exempla (London, 1555; not in
STC). See Jordan, The Threshold of Power, p. 409.

791-95. in Melancthon's . . . Latine] Although Edward
probably did undertake these studies, most contemporary
sources and later writers attribute these specific readings
and translations to Elizabeth. Camden is Heywood's source
here, and his statement is so similar that one must suspect
Heywood of either confusing or deliberately rearranging
Camden: "With Roger Ascham . . . she read the Common places
of Melancthon, all Cicero, a great part of the History of
Titus Livius, the choice Orations of Isocrates (wherof she
translated two into Latine) . . ." (William Camden, Annales:
The True and Royall History of . . . Elizabeth [STC 4497;
1625], sigs. A1r-v). Ascham himself reports that "she read
with me almost all Cicero, and great part of Titus Livius.
. . . To these I added Saint Cyprian and Melanchthon's
Common Places . . . " (Ascham, p. lxiii). For a detailed
account of the classical education of Edward and Elizabeth
see T. W. Baldwin, William Shakespere's Small Latine & Lesse
Greeke (Urbana: Univ. of Illinois Press, 1944), I, 200-84.

791-92. Melancthon's common-places] The Loci communes
rerum theologicarum of Philip Melanchthon (1496-1560), first
published in 1521, with editions printed in Wittenberg and in
Basel, "was the first systematic presentation of evangelical
Protestant theology" (Clyde L. Manschreck, trans. and ed.,
Melanchthon on Christian Doctrine: Loci communes 1555 [New
York: Oxford Univ. Press, 1965], p. xxiii). During the
author's lifetime it went through a great many editions and
translations and was often enlarged and revised by Melanchthon
himself, so that it is impossible to know which version either
Edward or Elizabeth may have used. According to Manschreck,
Elizabeth "memorized large portions of it in order to converse
learnedly about theology" and "directed scholars to read
Melanchthon 'to induce them to all godliness'" (pp. xx, xxi).

793-94. two of Isocrates Orations] The two translations
done by Elizabeth were identified by John Bale as the second
and third orations to Nicoles. See T. W. Baldwin, I, 261.

801. sidenote: Peter Heylyn's The historie of St. George (STC 13272; 1631) was entered in the Stationers' Register on 8 November 1630. Heywood probably read it in manuscript.

804. Legenda aurea] Jacobus de Vorgine's popular Legenda aurea (STC 24873 et seq.) was first printed by Caxton in 1483 and went through a number of editions through 1527.

820-30. Lord . . . sake.] In almost identical language, including the "dying words," this prayer was printed as a broadside entitled The Prayer of Kynge Edwarde the syxte . . . (STC 7509). It is undated and may have appeared shortly after Edward's death, but its direct appeal to "defend this Land from Papistry, and maintaine thy true Religion," would have placed the printer, Richard Jugge, in a dangerous position. It may have been printed after Mary's reign; Jugge died in 1577.

833. suspition of poyson] There is no evidence to substantiate such a suspicion, but the rumor was current in London and abroad (see Jordan, The Threshold of Power, p. 520, n. 1). There were also stories that Edward had not died at all; one such rumor surfaced as late as 1599 (Margaret E. Cornford, "A Legend concerning Edward VI," English Historical Review, 23 [1908], 286-90).

872. Hic iacet] "Here lies"; i.e., the initial words on a tombstone.

886. prima ibi ante omnes] "Then, foremost of all." Virgil, The Aeneid, II, 40.

889. Lord Courtney] Edward Courtenay (1526?-1556). In 1538, Henry Courtenay was accused of treason and sent to the Tower with his wife Gertrude Blount (Elizabeth's godmother) and their son Edward. Henry was executed and his wife was released, but Edward remained in the Tower until 1553. Under Mary he was created Earl of Devonshire and carried the sword of state at the coronation. He courted Mary and, later, Elizabeth. For his part in Wyatt's rebellion he was imprisoned briefly and then, in 1555, released and exiled. He died in Padua.

892. Gardiner] Stephen Gardiner (1483?-1555), Bishop of Winchester, became private secretary to Wolsey circa 1526. He performed a number of ambassadorial tasks and gradually worked his way into the favor of the king, who gave him his see and

whom he served as ambassador to France and Germany on several
occasions. He was chief celebrant of the mass at Henry's
funeral. He was imprisoned during most of Edward's reign and
replaced in his bishopric by John Poynet. Released at Mary's
accession, "he was made lord high chancellor of the realm, and
in this capacity placed the crown on her head at her coronation . . . and presided at the opening of parliament." Although generally held responsible for the intensity of the
Marian persecutions, he made efforts to save the lives of
Cranmer and Northumberland and to prevent the imprisonment of
Peter Martyr. Earlier in life, he had worked diligently on
Henry's divorce, but under Mary he advocated having the divorce declared invalid and Elizabeth illegitimate. "His whole
treatment of Elizabeth . . . remains, indeed, one of the most
sinister features in his later career, and it is asserted that
after Wyatt's conspiracy he meditated her removal by foul
means."

892. John Poynet] or Ponet (1514?-1556). At one time
Cranmer's chaplain, later (1550) Bishop of Rochester and, in
the next year, translated to Winchester. He died in exile
at Strasburg.

893. Bonner] Edmund Bonner (1500?-1569). On 1 October
1549 Bonner was sentenced to life imprisonment in Marshalsea
by the Archbishop of Canterbury, for refusing to state in a
Paul's Cross sermon on 1 September that Edward's authority was
no less in his minority than it would be if he were an adult.
He was released on 5 August 1553. In July 1559 he refused to
take the oath of supremacy and was returned to Marshalsea,
where he died (DNB; Wriothesley, II, 24, 96, 145).

894. John Day] George Day (1501?-1556) became Bishop of
Chichester in 1543. He was imprisoned in 1550 for preaching
against the illegal destruction of altars, deprived of his
bishopric the following year, and restored shortly after
Mary's accession. He preached at Edward's funeral and at
Mary's accession.

894. John Scory] (d. 1585); Bishop of Rochester (1551)
and Chichester (1552). "On Mary's accession Scory was deprived, but submitted himself to Bonner, renounced his wife,
did penance for being married, and . . . was allowed to offi-
ciate in the London diocese." He went into voluntary exile
shortly thereafter, returning to England at Elizabeth's
accession. In 1559 he became Bishop of Hereford.

895. Tonstall] Cuthbert Tunstall (1474-1559), Bishop of

London (1522-1530) and Durham (1530-59), and one of the most
highly respected scholars and ecclesiastics of his time. A
moderate Catholic, he was imprisoned in 1551, charged (almost
certainly falsely) with abetting a northern rebellion. Under
Mary he served on several commissions to examine Protestant
bishops, but, although most were deprived, Tunstall never
actively persecuted any nor did he condemn any to death.

895. Heath] Nicholas Heath (1501?-1578), Bishop of
Rochester in 1539, translated to Worcester in 1543. He and
Tunstall were the official censors and readers of the Great
Bible. Deprived of his see and briefly imprisoned in the
Fleet for refusing a form for ordination which called for re-
placing altars with tables, he was reinstated at Mary's accession and elected Archbishop of York in 1555. Upon Mary's
death, Heath, as chancellor, proclaimed Elizabeth's accession
in the House of Lords. He continued to serve under Elizabeth
until 1559, when, for refusing the Oath of Supremacy, he was
deprived of his see and committed to the Tower for a short
period. He spent the remainder of his life in retirement.

896. John Hooper] (d. 1555); Bishop of Gloucester and
Worcester. Hooper fled England in 1539 to avoid persecution,
then returned in 1549 to become chaplain to Protector Somerset. He was sent to the Fleet for a brief time in 1551 for
his refusal to wear episcopal vestments at his consecration.
Although he supported Mary against Jane Grey's faction, he
was arrested soon after her succession; refusing to recant,
he was burnt in Gloucester on 9 February 1555. "By his actions and writings Hooper very effectively contributed to the
popularizing of extreme puritanic views of religion in
England."

897. Vesey] John Veysey or Voysey (1465?-1554),
Dean of Windsor (1515-19), Dean of Wolverhampton (1516-21),
and Bishop of Exeter from 1519 until he was removed in 1551.

897. Miles Coverdale] (1488-1568). Coverdale is perhaps
best known for his translations of the Bible. His first complete version was published on the continent in 1535 and
brought into England the same year; it went into a second edition in 1537. In 1538 he was sent to Paris by Cromwell to
oversee the production of the Great Bible, eventually comp-
pleted in London in 1539. During his exile (1553-59) he and
William Whittingham began a new Protestant Bible, the New
Testament appearing in 1557; this was the first version to be
set in roman type and to number the verses.

899. dissemble] "To put on a feigned or false appearance of; to feign, pretend, simulate" (OED).

944. assayed] assay: "To try with afflictions, temptations, force, etc. In some senses apparently influenced by assail" (OED).

974. Statists] "politicians"

1021. Booke] A collection of prayers now in the British Library (MS.Harl.2342) may be the book she carried. It was apparently used to convey messages, as there are three notes in the book: one from Guilford Dudley to his father the Duke of Suffolk; one from Jane Grey to her father; and one from Jane Grey to John Brydges, Lieutenant of the Tower. J. G. Nichols conjectures that the book may have belonged to Brydges (The Chronicle of Queen Jane, and of Two Years of Queen Mary, ed. John Gough Nichols, Camden Society [1850; rpt. New York: AMS, 1968], p. 57, note d).

1021. Mr. Bridges] Sir John Brydges (1490?-1556), a staunch Catholic, was made Lieutenant of the Tower on Mary's accession. He helped quell Wyatt's rebellion and had charge of Wyatt (whom he used rather harshly) in the Tower. He was kind and lenient with both Jane Grey and Elizabeth. He was in charge of the executions of Wyatt and Hooper. In April 1554 he was created first Baron Chandos of Sudeley, and in June he gave over his position in the Tower to his brother Thomas.

1040. Judge Morgan] Sir Richard Morgan, a Roman Catholic, joined the Princess Mary immediately after the death of Edward VI. "Though he does not seem to have been a well-known lawyer, he was at once promoted in his profession. He was a commissioner to hear Bishop Tunstall's appeal against his conviction in June [1553], was created chief justice of the common pleas in September, and was knighted on 2 Oct." He resigned the bench in October 1555 and died the following summer.

1052. praecellent] "surpassing, pre-eminent." OED gives only the spelling "precellent." In The Exemplary Lives and memorable Acts of nine the most worthy Women of the World (STC 13316; 1640) Heywood wrote, of Elizabeth: "Nay, what praecelling vertue soever, was commendable in any one particular, or all in generall, may, without flattery be justly conferred on her" (sig. 2B1r).

1080. her workes] These three works and her "last words"

were collected as The Life, Death and Actions of the Lady Jane
Grey (STC 7281; 1615). They were reprinted in Foxe (VI, 425-
22) and in The Harleian Miscellany (III, 112-19).

1081. Epistle to Mr. Harding] Presumably STC 7279, An
Epistle of the Ladye Jane to a Learned Man. . . . In Life,
Death and Actions (see note to l. 1080) it is entitled simply
"An admonition to such as are weake in faith." Thomas Harding
(1516-1572) was chaplain to Jane's father, Henry Grey, and an
early tutor to Jane in religion. Although a zealous Protestant, under Mary he "accepted the Romish views with ardour,
and probably with sincerity." It was this expedient conversion which prompted Jane's "epistle." At Elizabeth's accession he refused to reconvert and fled to Louvain, from whence
he carried on a heated controversy with Bishop John Jewel.

1083. Renegado] "Renegade," in the sense of a deserter
or traitor. Heywood used the term earlier in a passage of
hissing, quasi-euphuistic rage: "Downe wth these Sacraligious
salsaparreales. these vnsanctiffied sarlaboyses: that woold
make a very Seralia off the sanctuary and are meare renegadoes
to all religion . . ." (The Captives, ed. Arthur Brown, Malone
Society [Oxford: Oxford Univ. Press, 1953], ll. 1509-12).

1085. Colloquy with Fecknam] Appended to An Epistle
. . . to a learned man (STC 7279), this seems not to have
been published separately. John de Feckenham (1518?-1585)
was Mary's private chaplain. Noted for his kindness, he
converted many Protestants (including John Cheke) and tried
to save the lives of those who remained unconverted. "Four
days before Lady Jane Grey's execution Feckenham was sent by
Mary to attempt her conversion, but he found it impossible
to shake her constancy, and finally, it is said, acknowledged
himself fitter to be her disciple than her master. . . . On
the scaffold he took leave of her with the words that he was
sorry for her, for he was sure they two would never meet."

1092. Duke of Buckingham] Henry Stafford (1454?-1482),
second Duke of Buckingham. An early supporter of Richard
III, Buckingham shortly after the coronation and for reasons
that are not entirely clear, raised an army against the
king. He was betrayed by his servant, one Ralph Bannister,
in whose cottage near Shrewsbury he was hiding.

1094. Underwood] Little is known of him beyond the
story Heywood tells. He was the gamekeeper of Suffolk's
estate of Astley Cooper, near Coventry, Warwickshire.

1104. Earle of <u>Huntington</u>] Francis Hastings (1514?-1561), second Earl of Huntingdon, joined Northumberland against Protector Somerset and in declaring for Lady Jane Grey, an act for which he spent six months in the Tower. At his release he was sent to capture Suffolk. He was married to Cardinal Pole's niece Catherine. "Although apparently pliable in religious matters, [he] was inclined to protestantism at heart."

1111-12. <u>paries</u> <u>nunc</u> <u>proximus</u> <u>ardet</u>] "Now that your neighbor's wall is burning." Cf. "nam tua res agitur, paries cum proximus ardet" (Horace, <u>Epistles</u>, I, 18, 84).

1120. butt] In archery, "a mound or other erection on which the target is set up" (<u>OED</u>); that is, the backing used to prevent the arrow from passing completely through the target, or "mark."

1139. <u>Raviliacke</u>] Francois Ravaillac (1578-1610) was a religious fanatic and the assassin of Henry IV of France. In the seventeenth century, his name became synonymous with treachery and perfidy. In 1641, e.g., Henry Parker wrote: "<u>Bastwick</u>, <u>Prin</u>, and <u>Burton</u> . . . are Names now as horrid in the World, as <u>Garnet</u>, <u>Faux</u>, <u>Ravilliack</u>" (<u>A</u> <u>Discourse</u> <u>Concerning</u> <u>Puritans</u> [Thomason tract E204(3)], sig. A4r).

1145-46] <u>Quocunque</u> . . . <u>aër</u>.] "Wherever I gaze there is naught but sea and air." Ovid, <u>Tristia</u>, I, ii, 23.

1149. stomack't] "To inspire with resentment, fury or courage; to incite" (<u>OED</u>).

1173. John <u>Williams</u>] (1500?-1559). He was knighted in 1537, served as keeper of the King's jewels from 1539 to 1544, and as member of parliament in 1542 and again from 1547 to 1554, and was created Baron Williams of Thame in 1554 (<u>DNB</u>). Heywood here follows Foxe's error in placing Williams on the scene. The third lord was, in fact, William Howard, Lord High Admiral and Elizabeth's great-uncle. Foxe (VIII, 606) also erroneously places Sir Richard Southwell here.

1174. Edward <u>Hastings</u>] Privy Councillor and Master of the Horse (d. 1573). Although regarded as a firm Catholic, he took the oath of supremacy after a brief imprisonment in 1561 for hearing mass.

1174-75. <u>Thomas</u> <u>Cornewallis</u>] (1519-1604); diplomat. He was commissioner at Wyatt's trial in 1554. As treasurer

of Calais (1554-57) he was thought by some to have sold it
to France. Appointed Comptroller of the Household in 1557,
he was removed from that office and from the Privy Council
at Elizabeth's accession.

1224-25. her Physitians] In fact, they were Mary's
physicians, Doctors Owen and Wendy (see note to ll. 2049-
50), who had been sent to Ashridge ahead of the commission
(Plowden, p. 157).

1235. Litter] "A vehicle . . . containing a couch shut
in by curtains, and carried on men's shoulders or by beasts
of burden," and "a framework supporting a bed or couch for
the transport of the sick and wounded" (OED).

1263. Ralph Rowlett] Little is known about Rowlet.
Nichols (in his edition of Machyn's Diary, p. 364) points
out the curious fact that he "buried two wives within seven
months" (actually eight months, between 8 December 1557 and
3 August 1558), and that "his father, also sir Ralph, had
been one of the masters of the mint to Henry VIII."
According to Thomas Hoby (cited by Nichols), Rowlet died in
St. Albans on 19 April 1571.

1265. Mr. Dod] unidentified. In a British Library copy
of Jean Froissart's Des Chroniques de France (Paris, 1513), is
bound a sheet of paper with manuscript notes on the children
of Henry Carey, first Lord Hunsdon. The notes may be in Hunsdon's hand. The fourth note reads: "Thomas Carey was borne
. . . yn the yere of our Lorde 1556: at northmyms in the
county of hertford Thomas parry and Mr Dods godfathers and my
lady pope godmuthar" (reprinted in F. H. Mares, ed., The
Memoirs of Robert Carey [Oxford: Clarendon Press, 1972],
p. 90). The date and location suggest that this may be the
same Mr. Dod.

1266. Hie-gate] Elizabeth stayed in Highgate at the
home of Sir Roger Cholmley (Plowden, p. 158). Cholmley (d.
1565) had been Recorder of London and Lord Chief Justice
before being fined heavily and sent to the Tower on 27 July
1553 for having witnessed the will of Edward VI.

1272-73. Lord Chamberlaine, and Sir John Gage] Heywood
is in error here; Gage was the Lord Chamberlain. According
to Foxe (VIII, 607), the two persons in attendance were Gage
and his Vice-chamberlain, perhaps Sir Henry Jerningham (d.
1571), Vice-chamberlain of the Household, captain of the
guard, and a great favorite of Mary's (DNB).

1278-81. Quo . . . est.] "Whither the Fates, in their
ebb and flow, draw us, let us follow; whatever befall, all
fortune is to be o'ercome by bearing." Vergil, The Aeneid,
V, 709-10.

1311. Nicholas Throckmorton] (1515-1571); knighted by
Edward whose succession document he signed. He supported
Jane Grey but reconciled himself to Mary. He was seriously
implicated in Wyatt's rebellion but was found innocent by a
jury. Throckmorton often visited Elizabeth at Hatfield and
soon after her accession was appointed ambassador to France.
Although an ardent Protestant, he admired Mary Queen of Scots
and believed she had a claim to the succession.

1312. James Crofts] or Croft (on the problem with his
name, see the Textual Notes) (d. 1590). He became deputy-
constable of the Tower in 1553 but was removed later the
same year for his involvement in Wyatt's conspiracy. Tried
and convicted, he was imprisoned in the Tower until January
1555, when (apparently having restored himself to Mary's
good graces) he was released. Under Elizabeth he was a
member of parliament and of the Privy Council and served as
commissioner at the trial of Mary Queen of Scots.

1316. Peter Carew] (1514-1575). A gentleman of the
Privy Chamber under Henry, "he opposed the attempt to place
Lady Jane Grey on the throne, and proclaimed Mary as queen
in the west." He opposed Mary's marriage to Philip and
tried to stop it. Having fled to the continent, he was
arrested in Antwerp, with Sir John Cheke, and sent to the
Tower. He won favor again at Elizabeth's accession.

1363-64. Earle of Sussex] Thomas Radcliffe, third Earl
of Sussex (1526?-1583), was appointed Lord Deputy of Ireland
by Mary and reappointed by Elizabeth. He assisted in negoti-
ating Mary's marriage with Philip and in trying to arrange
Elizabeth's marriage to the Duke of Anjou and the Duke of
Alencon.

1371-72. Flebile . . . sequatur.] "The end of a thing
is better then the beginning thereof." Ecclesiastes 7:10;
Geneva Bible.

1378. Gutta cavat lapidem] "By constant dripping water
hollows stone." Ovid, Epistolae ex Ponto, IV, 10, 5; but perhaps proverbial. The metaphor is not uncommon in Elizabethan
literature; cf., e.g., Thomas Sackville's personification of
sorrow in the "Induction" to The Mirror for Magistrates

(1563) (ed. Lily B. Campbell [Cambridge: Cambridge Univ.
Press, 1938], p. 301): "And as the stone that droppes of water
weares, / So dented were her cheekes with fall of teares."

1383. Non . . . occidit] "Thy sunne shal never go
downe." Isaiah 60:20; Geneva Bible.

1387. two Lords] The Earl of Sussex and the Marquis of
Winchester (William Paulet, first Baron St. John and Lord
High Treasurer).

1400. apperill] "peril, risk." Shakespeare: "Let me
stay at thine apperil, Timon" (Timon, I, ii, 33). Jonson
uses the term several times: "Faith I will baile him, at
mine owne apperill" (Magnetic Lady, V, x, 50; cf. Devil Is
an Ass, V, iv, 34, and Tale of a Tub, II, ii, 93).

1405. writing] Elizabeth's letter to Mary protesting
her innocence is reproduced in facsimile and transcription
in Frank A. Mumby, The Girlhood of Queen Elizabeth: A
Narrative in Contemporary Letters (London: Constable, 1909),
pp. 115-17.

1471-72. her Gentleman-Usher] Bedingfield identifies
Elizabeth's gentleman-usher during her stay at Woodstock as
one "Cornwallys." Exactly who this was and for how long he
held this position I have been unable to determine. See
C. R. Manning, ed., "State Papers Relating to the Custody
of the Princess Elizabeth at Woodstock in 1554," Norfolk
Archaeology, 4 (1855), 133-231, hereafter cited as
"Bedingfield Papers." Most of these letters are reproduced,
after quite heavy "editing," by Mumby (pp. 127-87).

1503-04. more strict watch] According to Mumby (p.
118) the suggestion for stricter measures was made by
Winchester.

1530. interressed] "interested"

1542. the Nobility] According to a letter from the
French ambassador Antoine de Noailles, Philip was met by
Arundel, Derby, Shrewsbury, Pembroke, and others, Arundel
presenting him with the Order of the Garter (quoted, in
part, in Chronicle of Queen Jane, p. 137, note c). The
earliest printed account of Philip's landing and marriage,
from which almost all later chroniclers draw, is John
Elder's The copie of a letter sent in to Scotlande, of the

<u>arivall</u> <u>of</u> <u>Philippe</u>, <u>Prynce</u> <u>of</u> <u>Spaine</u> (STC 7552; 1555;
reprinted in <u>Chronicle</u> <u>of</u> <u>Queen</u> <u>Jane</u>, pp. 137-66). Martin
A. S. Hume ("The Visit of Philip II," <u>English</u> <u>Historical</u>
<u>Review</u>, 7 [1892], 253-80) presents an interesting account of
the landing, drawn from contemporary Spanish sources.
According to these accounts, Pembroke was not present at
Philip's landing but arrived the following day (266). Hume
takes Noailles to task for being an unreliable reporter as
well as a man of singularly poor judgment (254-56).

1549. Caparison'd] Caparisons were the trappings and
riggings (often highly ornate) of a horse.

1553. honourably attended] According to the Spanish
sources which Hume examined, when Philip left Southampton
for Winchester he "was surrounded by the English nobles
Winchester, Arundel, Derby, Worcester, Bedford, Rutland,
Pembroke, Surrey, Clinton, Cogham, Willoughby, Darcy,
Maltraves, Talbot, Strange, Fitzwalter, and North" ("Visit
of Philip II," 269).

1560-61. Bishop of that Sea] Stephen Gardiner

1584. Lord <u>Steward</u>] Henry Fitzalan (1511?-1580),
twelfth earl of Arundel, served as lord-deputy of Calais
from 1540 to 1543. He was Lord Chamberlain and a member of
the Privy Council under Edward until ousted by Warwick.
Under Mary he was reinstated to the Council and made Lord
Steward of the Household, positions in which he continued
under Elizabeth. By 1564 he had fallen out of favor with
the queen and gave up his stewardship; he became one of the
leaders of the Catholic movement to replace Elizabeth with
Mary Stuart, and was imprisoned for his part in the Ridolphi
plot.

1584-85. Earles of <u>Derby</u> and <u>Pembrooke</u>] Edward Stanley
(1508-1572), third Earl of Derby, was a Privy Councillor under Henry, Mary, and Elizabeth, and served as a special commissioner at the trial of Jane Grey. William Herbert (1501?-
1570), first Earl of Pembroke of the second creation, was a
gentleman of the Privy Council under Henry and a member of
the Council and Master of the Horse under Edward. He commanded the forces which put down Wyatt's rebellion and in 1556
was appointed Governor of Calais.

1615. consummate] "Of marriage: = consummated" (<u>OED</u>).

1627. Countees] in the sense of "counts," sometimes

spelled "contes." OED lists "countee" as an obsolete form of
"county," which is apparently what 32 read it as.

1702. Lord Shandoys] Sir John Brydges, Baron Chandos.
See note to 1. 1021.

1709. Daedalus] "A skilful or cunning artificer" (OED).
Daedalus built the intricately confusing labyrinth in which
King Minos hid the Minotaur.

1720-21. Henry Benningfield] usually spelled
"Bedingfield" (1511-1583). One of the first to declare
Mary's right to the throne upon the death of Edward, he was
made Privy Councillor upon her accession. He was in charge
of Elizabeth from May 1554 to June 1555 and seems to have
made a tentative peace with her after her accession.

1836. Deane of Windsor] William Franklyn (1480?-1556)
was appointed Dean of Windsor in December 1536. In 1540 he
took occupancy of the rectory of Chalfont St. Giles, Bucking-
hamshire.

1837. Dormers house] The home of Sir William Dormer,
son of Robert Baron Dormer of Wyng (now West Wycombe), Buck-
inghamshire (Plowden, p. 175). William was made Knight of
the Bath at the accession of Mary (Machyn, p. 334), and died
in 1616 (DNB, see "Dormer, Jane"). His daughter, Jane, was a
close childhood companion of Mary.

1840. Tame his house] At Ricote, in Oxfordshire (Foxe,
VIII, 615, n. 2).

1849. after-clappes] "An unexpected stroke after the re-
cipient has ceased to be on his guard; a subsequent surprise"
(OED). Oenone tells Paris: "Loue me, and so preuent all
after-clappes" (Oenone and Paris, 1. 96).

1858. Erostratus] or Herostratus. Beyond this story,
nothing seems to be known of him. He burnt the Temple of
Artemis in the city of Ephesus; legend has it that he
committed his act on the day Alexander the Great was born
(Oxford Companion to Classical Literature, ed. Paul Harvey
[Oxford: Clarendon Press, 1937], p. 160).

1876-77. Keeper of the house] Foxe names "one Paul Peny,
a keeper of Woodstock, a notorious ruffian and a butcherly
wretch," who "was appointed to kill . . . Elizabeth" (VIII,

618). Foxe neither identifies him further nor says who "appointed" him.

1886. worthy Knight] Perhaps one of the following, named in a letter of 27 May 1554 from Bedingfield to the Privy Council: "I have founde verye moche diligence in Sir John Broune [sheriff of Oxfordshire], Sir John Harecourte, and Syr Wylliam Raynsfurth, to be redye to serve the quenes Majestie uppon occasion nedefull ("Bedingfield Papers," 162).

1888. liberty of the Gardens] Bedingfield explained his duty in a letter to the Lord Chamberlain: "hir grace to have libertee to walke in the Gardeyn whensoever she doth commaunde . . . eyther my lorde Shandoes or I . . . to geve our attendaunce at that tyme" ("Bedingfield Papers," 141).

1899-1900. _humus_ _aut_ _humi_ _repens_] "Earth returns to earth."

1924. burned] In a postscript to his letter of 27 May 1554 to the Council, Bedingfield says: "There was sum peryll off fyer within the house, which we have, withoute eny losse to be regarded, escaped, thanks be unto god" ("Bedingfield Papers," 163). Mumby (p. 139) is surely correct in his comment that "Bedingfield's postscript . . . probably provides the key to the mystery of the fire which developed, in the narratives of Foxe and Heywood, into a dastardly attempt to burn Elizabeth in her bed!" I have found no other contemporary reference to either the fire or the "worthy Knight" (1. 1928; cf. 1886) who extinguished it. Foxe, of course, seldom passed up the opportunity, however slight, of linking a good fire and a good Protestant.

2049-50. Dr. _Owen_ and Dr. _Wendye_] George _Owen_ (d. 1558) and Thomas Wendy (1500?-1560) were physicians to Henry VIII, Edward, and Mary.

2105. _Basset_] James Basset was, according to Foxe, "one of the privy-chamber, a great man about the queen, and chief darling of Stephen Gardiner" (VIII, 618). Royall Tyler describes him as "son of Sir Jn. Basset and Honor Grenville (later Lady Lisle). He was taken into Gardiner's service as a youth, and became Chamberlain to Queen Mary. . . . He was one of Gardiner's executors" (Tyler, ed. _Calendar_ _of_ _State_ _Papers_ _Spanish_, vol. 12 [London: HMSO, 1949], p. 242, n). Machyn takes note of his funeral: "The xxvj day of November [1558] was bered at the Blake Frers in Smythfeld master Bassett sqwyre, on[e] of the chambur with quen Mare . . ."

194

(<u>Diary</u>, p. 179).

2148. <u>Edmond Tremaine</u>] (d. 1582). A Devonshire man in
the service of Edward Courtenay, Tremayne was sent to the
Tower in 1554 under suspicion of being involved in Wyatt's
rebellion. Foxe (VIII, 619) is the apparent originator of
the story of Tremayne's racking. Released from prison early
in 1555, he seems to have joined Courtenay in Italy. By 1561
he had returned to England. In 1571 he was made Clerk of the
Privy Council, and the next year was M. P. for Plymouth (<u>DNB</u>).

2148. Mr. <u>Smithweeke</u>] Probably one of the Wyatt
conspirators. One William Smethwick was sent to the Tower
in February 1554 and then transferred to the Fleet in June
(<u>Chronicle of Queen Jane</u>, pp. 53, 71n).

2159-60. <u>Henry Chamberlaine</u>] Foxe gives the name as
Ralph (VIII, 610), but Wriothesley (II, 116) reports it cor-
rectly as Leonard. He served occasional terms as sheriff of
Oxfordshire and Berkshire and was knighted the day following
Mary's coronation. As an officer of the Tower from 1549 to
1553, he was probably the one who received the prisoners from
Wyatt's rebellion. In 1553 he was made governor of Guernsey,
where he died in August 1561.

2192. <u>Shrewsbury</u>, and <u>Secretary Peter</u>] Francis Talbot
(1500-1560), fifth Earl of Shrewsbury, whose eldest son,
George, was the keeper of Mary Queen of Scots; William Petre
(1505?-1572), Secretary of State from 1543 to 1566.

2297. <u>Thomas Pope</u>] (1507?-1559). Founder, the previous year, of Trinity College, Oxford.

2300-01. <u>in libera custodia</u>] "house arrest"

2326. Bishop <u>Ridley</u> and Master <u>Latimer</u>] Nicholas Ridley
(1500?-1555), Bishop of Rochester and London, and Hugh Latimer
(1485?-1555), Bishop of Worcester, perhaps the two most famous
Protestant martyrs. Ridley was sent to the Tower in June 1553
for preaching a Paul's Cross sermon which promoted Lady Jane
Grey and branded both Mary and Elizabeth as bastards. Latimer
went to the Tower upon Mary's accession. With Cranmer, they
were sent to Oxford in 1554 to debate their religious views
with the divines of the university; as a result of the debate
all three were declared heretics and sent to the stake, Ridley and Latimer together on 16 October 1555 and Cranmer five
months later (<u>DNB</u>). Heywood's description of them as "those
two bright shining lamps" (1. 2325) recalls Latimer's final

words as the two men were at the stake: "Be of good comfort, master Ridley, and play the man. We shall this day light such a candle, by God's grace, in England, as I trust shall never be put out" (Foxe, VII, 50).

2373. Pistolets] A pistolet was a small gold coin. A royal proclamation of 2 November 1560 (STC 7919) gives its value as five shillings and ten pence.

2378. poin'd] Perhaps used metaphorically to mean "burst" or "proven false." OED gives "to prick; to harass, annoy" which may apply; the only example cited with this sense is from the fourteenth century.

2383. Timpany] "Sometimes used vaguely for a morbid swelling or tumour of any kind" (OED; "tympany"). Both Holinshed and Camden use the term in describing Mary's death.

2419. way] An obsolete form of "weigh" still in use in the seventeenth century (OED).

2424. moderne] "Every-day, ordinary, commonplace" (OED, def. A.4). In this sense it provides the necessary antithetical balance with "forraigne" (1. 2423) for which Heywood was obviously striving. OED cites examples from Lodge, Shakespeare, and Jonson, but the editor of 32 apparently was not familiar with this meaning of the term and thus emended it to "hombred" ("homebred" in 41).

2436. Cardinall Poole] Reginald Pole (1500-1558), Cardinal and Archbishop of Canterbury. Although originally in Henry's service he tried first to remain neutral over the divorce question and then to deter Henry. Much of his life was spent trying to restore the papal supremacy which Henry irrevocably destroyed. From 1532 to 1554 Pole lived in Italy where, in 1549, he very nearly won election to succeed Pope Paul III. Before Philip left England in 1555 he put Pole in charge of caring for Mary. He succeeded Cranmer as Archbishop of Canterbury and was soon after elected chancellor of both Oxford and Cambridge. During the war between Pope Paul IV and Philip, Pole fell out of favor with the pope and was deprived of his legateship. He died just twelve hours after Mary, on 17 November.

2441. sidenote: I have been unable to find a source for the number 260; perhaps it is given in Foxe. In any case, the sum of the individual figures given in this passage is

341. Most modern historians place the figure at around 300.

2443. Artificers] Intended here in the sense of "craftsmen."

2453-54. Quis . . . lachrimis?] "Who could in telling such a tale refrain from tears?" Virgil, The Aeneid, II, 6-8.

2460-61. Martyn Bucer and Paulus Phagius] Bucer (1491-1551) and Fagius (1504-1549) were Protestant divines who fled from the continent to England in 1549. Both went to Cambridge, Bucer as Professor of Divinity and Fagius as a Reader in Hebrew.

2466. Peter Martirs wife] Peter Martyr (Pietro Martire Vermigli, 1500-1562) was a Protestant divine and reformer brought to England by Cranmer in 1547. His wife, one Catherine Cathie, an ex-nun, was buried in Christ Church Cathedral in 1553 and was reinterred in 1558.

2497-99. At . . . venis.] "But the queen, long since smitten with a grievous love-pang, feeds the wound with her life-blood." Virgil, The Aeneid, IV, 1-2.

2518. sidenote: Henry actually died early in the morning of 28 January 1547, a Friday (Pollard, p. 340).

2522. sidenote: "Not fierce by nature but because of the craft of bishops."

2525. sidenote: "The bloddie, & deceitful men shal not live halfe their dayes." Psalms 55:23; Geneva Bible.

2531. Lucius] Mythical king of Britain; see Geoffrey of Monmouth, The History of the Kings of Britain, iv, 19. "The Lucius story turns up throughout Elizabethan literature" (Yates, "Queen Elizabeth as Astraea," 71).

2590. the Seate of worthy Governement] This pageant is described in detail in a contemporary account of the royal passage through London, The Quenes maiesties passage through the citie of London to westminster the daye before her coronacion (STC 7591; ed. Arthur F. Kinney, in Elizabethan Backgrounds [Hamden, Conn.: Archon, 1975], pp. 7-39). In part, the description reads as follows: "In the front of the same pageant was written the name and title therof, which is The seate of worthie governance, which seate was made in such artificiall maner, as to the apperance of the lookers on,

the foreparte semed to have no staie, and therfore of force
was stayed by lively personages, which personages were in num-
bre foure . . . eche having his face to the Quene and people,
wherof every one had a table to expresse their effectes,
which are vertues, namelie Pure religion, Love of subjectes,
Wisedome and Justice, which did treade their contrarie vices
under their feete, that is to witte, Pure religion, did treade
uppon Superstition, and Ignoraunce, Love of subjectes, did
tread upon Rebellion and Insolencie, Wisedome did treade upon
follie and vaine glorie, Justice did treade upon Adulacion
and Briberie. Eche of these personages according to their
proper names and properties, had not onlie their names in
plaine, and perfit writing set upon their breastes easelie to
be read of all, but also every of them was aptelie and
properlie apparelled, so that his apparell and name did agre
to expresse the same person, that in title he represented"
(p. 22). There is a discussion of The Quenes maiesties
passage and of the pageants in David M. Bergeron, English
Civic Pageantry 1558-1642 (Columbia: Univ. of South Carolina
Press, 1971), pp. 12-23. Of the pamphlet, Bergeron writes
that "it was also a text that Heywood knew well when he
wrote Englands Elizabeth" (p. 13); it is just as likely that
Heywood took it from Holinshed, who reprinted the pamphlet
verbatim (IV, 158-76).

2611. John Perrot] Perrot (1527?-1592) was rumored to
be the son of Henry VIII and Mary Berkely. He was created
Knight of the Bath by Edward. Under Mary, he spent a brief
time in the Fleet, accused of sheltering heretics, then
fought under Pembroke in France. He served in Ireland for
many years, and died in the Tower, accused of treason for
having spoken contemptuously of Elizabeth and her council.
There is an account of him in Robert Naunton's Fragmenta
Regalia, ed. Edward Arber, English Reprints series (London:
1870).

2621. sidenote: Geoffrey Boleyn, father of William Boleyn, grandfather of Thomas Boleyn, great-grandfather of Anne
Boleyn, was Lord Mayor of London in 1457 (Plowden, p. 23).
He was thus one generation further removed from Elizabeth
than Heywood has him--he was her great-grandfather's father.

2636. her brothers foundation] Inspired by a sermon on
charity delivered by Bishop Ridley, Edward "felt a sense of
direct responsibility for the care of London's poor," and
with the cooperation of the Lord Mayor, the aldermen, and a
number of leading citizens had Christ's Hospital (primarily
an orphanage) built; it opened 23 November 1552 (Jordan, The

<u>Threshold</u> <u>of</u> <u>Power</u>, pp. 219-20). Heywood's source here was probably Holinshed (III, 1060-62).

2646-47. <u>Est</u> . . . <u>piam</u>.] "It is because she reigns that she has been pious."

DATE DUE

16 May 83			